JOHN PERKINS:
Land Where My Father Died

Gordon D. Aeschliman

Regal Books
A Division of GL Publications
Ventura, California, U.S.A.

Published by Regal Books
A Division of GL Publications
Ventura, California 93006
Printed in U.S.A.

Library of Congress Cataloging-in-Publication Data

Aeschliman, Gordon D., 1957-
  John Perkins, land where my father died.

    1. Perkins, John, 1930-   . 2. Afro-Americans—Mississippi—Biography.
3. Christian biography—Mississippi. 4. Mississippi—Race Relations. I. Title.
E185.97.P48A64   1987   280'.4 [B]   87-12700
ISBN 0-8307-1075-2

2 3 4 5 6 7 8 9 / 99 98 97 96 95 94 93 92

Rights for publishing this book in other languages are contracted by Gospel
Literature International (GLINT). GLINT also provides technical help for
the adaptation, translation, and publishing of Bible study resources and
books in scores of languages worldwide. For further information, contact
GLINT, Post Office Box 488, Rosemead, California, 91770, U.S.A., or the
publisher.

Cover photograph and photos appearing on pp. 2, 3, 12, 22, 26, 50, 56, 62,
63, 69, 78, 88, 96, 113, 120, 140, 154, 163, 164 are courtesy of Bob
Anderson/Life Productions. Used by permission. Photograph on p. 175
courtesy of the White House, Washington, D.C. Used by permission. Other
photos courtesy of the John M. Perkins Foundation for Reconciliation and
Development. Used by permission.

Contents

Preface

L*AND WHERE MY FATHER DIED*, shares the personal and intimate circumstances in my life which God has used to refine and prepare me for His glory and service. The opening scene on the railroad track with my father depicts the beginning of a life-long search for love and belonging. Even at four years of age, a very conscious longing for my father was both deep and overwhelming. My own heartache also reflects the heartache of those thousands of other young blacks born in the ghettos of this nation with no father at home.

My story depicts three basic inherited human needs. One is the need to belong and to be wanted. Of course, this need is best satisfied in a family household, where there is a mother and a father who wants you. This is the foundation for human development, and no person, government program or agent, regardless of how well intended, can ever replace that need for the family.

The second inherited need is for significance and importance. The need for dignity is planted in every human being and is forever crying out for the affirmation that I am somebody. When this affirmation is not received, human growth is severely limited.

The third human need requires a reasonable amount of security and safety. When this need is not met the result is a life of fear—one of the most powerful human emotions.

Again, a strong family environment meets this need for provision. Thus, it is easy to see that my childhood lacked all three basic needs.

My mother died when I was just seven months old. My father was devastated and gave the five of us away to his mother. She in turn gave away two to another family member. My older brother was killed by a policeman in a racial incident after returning from World War II. My sister was killed by her boyfriend, so I was left alone to try to find a sense of belonging and significance.

My inner search continued until 1957 when I met Jesus Christ in a little storefront mission in Pasadena, California. One Sunday morning I heard the preacher proclaim that God was my father and I could become a part of the family of God. That was good news to me that morning; I had found a reason for living, and I embraced that hope with all my heart. My life was transformed.

Soon a new ache began in me to go back home to Mississippi and express to the people back there that I had found a Father, and that He can be their father too. The first 12 years of my struggle was in Mendenhall. I saw the homeless, the hurting, the poor, and I realized that my new Father must have a concern for these people which means that I must have a concern for them too.

This new concern led us to begin a day-care center, a gym, a playground, a housing co-op, cooperative store, health center and a church. I wanted the people to see God's love so they could learn to love the God whom I loved. Today, people like Dolphus and Rosie Weary, Artis and Carolyn Fletcher, Jimmy Walker, Melvin Anderson and many others are still working to make God's love visible in Mississippi.

This growing concern eventually led me to Jackson, Mississippi for 10 years and then back to Pasadena where

I currently reside. The visible love of God must reach to all people, and I needed to find out if our philosophy would work in other places as well. If you could visit all three of those locations today, as well as other locations who have modeled our ministries, I believe you would see that the basic principles of Christian community development which we have learned will indeed stand the test of time.

The three principles which my life and ministry have been based on are: (1) relocation, (2) reconciliation (3) redistribution. Many effective models of ministry are working today that have followed these principles. The John M. Perkins Foundation for Reconciliation and Development in Pasadena, was created to challenge and educate these community-based ministries. If you would like more information, please write to me at 1581 Navarro Avenue, Pasadena, CA 91103.

1

"Your Daddy's Home"

GOOD GOD! If it ain' John Perkin. John Perkin! I been prayin' to God to send me Jesus and He send me John Perkin!"

Effie's 83-year-old body shuffled to the screen door and she thrust her crumpled face into the daylight to make sure she was seeing right.

"Heh, heh, Jesus. If it ain' John Perkin. Yep. John Perkin."

We arrange the chairs on the little porch attached to her house and listen to Effie recount the early days of John Perkins' ministry.

D'Lo, Mississippi is a rural town of no more than a few hundred blacks. Originally a logging station set in a swamp, D'Lo was first named "Damned Low." When formally registered as a town of Mississippi the name had to be changed to the more tasteful title, D'Lo, but that made no difference to the plight of its poverty-stricken residents who still suffered under the distasteful racism of the South.

Apparently, Effie prays a lot for Jesus to come and visit her. She'd been praying that in 1960 when John Perkins knocked at her door. John told her that he wanted to hold a

Bible study for anyone interested in learning more about Jesus. Effie immediately invited him in, and within weeks most of D'Lo was attending the weekly study held in a big tent on the plot next to Effie's home.

"When you came you were Jesus and we welcomed you," Effie said. "You told us the truth and it set us free from sin."

John preached very simply that Jesus wanted to live inside everyone and take care of them. "All the young folk followed him like a person offering whiskey," Effie recalls. "They liked his doctrine."

Effie and a few of her friends who were "noble people and loved God" had been hoping for a long time that someone would come and make a difference in the community. Blacks were economically oppressed and couldn't see a way out. They always gave in to white demands because there was no other way to feed the kids.

"Ezekiel saw the Messiah coming. Roads made straight, mountains made flat, valleys brought up. Good God! Jesus sent us John Perkin!"

Effie clapped her hands with delight as she described the wise men who visited baby Jesus in Bethlehem. "When you see Jesus you don't go back the same way no more." Back to D'Lo, "Hey, heh, we can't go on the same way no more after we seen Jesus!"

Shortly after his conversion in Monrovia, California, John was discipled by Wayne Lietch, a Vacation Bible School teacher who spent several hours each day with him studying the Bible. And that's exactly what John did in D'Lo. Soon the children began to change outwardly by giving up on certain "social" evils. They were dubbed "Perkins' kids."

Ethel Lee ("Ba Ba") lives a few hundred yards down from Effie, and he well remembers those early days. "A

66

I looked back
but Daddy was already gone.
And with him went my newfound joy
in belonging, in being loved,
in being somebody
for just a little while.
Years would pass
before I would know this joy again.

99

man from God named John was sent to us." Ba Ba rocked in his chair and laughed with the same fond "heh, heh" used by Effie. "John preached to us from the Word and told us that God was concerned about our being hungry, being outdoors, not being free."

Ba Ba had been a Baptist deacon for several years when he met John at those early tent meetings where he finally "got converted."

"John told us that we had to live differently. Had to care about our neighbor. God was concerned with *all* of me; I must be concerned with *all* of others."

But John didn't just preach the Word in D'Lo; he lived it. "He was a common man among common people," Ba Ba told me. "A little man. He would walk down the streets, never overlooked anybody, would give anything to anyone."

With a monthly income of only $400, John still modeled the message. Lucille, a 16-year-old, and her nine siblings were abandoned by their mother and a heavy burden on their father. John and Vera Mae helped care for them.

A couple of neighbors living under the strain of scarce finances began to fight about money that disappeared. John paid the missing money to bring peace. He helped residents apply for Farmers Home Administration (FHA) loans, organized voter registration drives, called on blacks to march together to show their solidarity and to boycott unfair businesses.

Soon D'Lo saw some changes with new houses being built and streets being paved. But not without a price to John. Imprisonment and threats became partners in his ministry. When given a "final order" by incensed whites to leave town, however, John found himself surrounded by friends who had found courage to say no to oppressors. "We told John to go inside and get some good sleep,"

BaBa told me. "We surrounded his house and stayed there until hostile feelings calmed down."

John is obviously in love with D'Lo even though it's been almost 25 years since ministering there. As we drive through the little town he points to each home and tells the story of the family.

"If you asked me to describe my life, to explain all the things I've been doing, I'd tell you in one word: parenting."

"Parenting" is a strange word to be sure when considering all of John's accomplishments: health centers, thrift stores, legal services, bands, churches, schools, construction companies and discipleship programs. But these are not the substance of what John has given his life to. They are simply the outward forms of a calling that was conceived deep inside the chest of a four-year-old. Hidden deep inside the frame of John Perkins is a painful, painful past. Rejection, loneliness and bitterness were childhood companions. The miracle of John Perkins is that those companions did not consume or crush him; rather, they became bridges to compassion.

John's life—in and around New Hebron, Mississippi—began in 1934 at four years old with the first time he recalls seeing his father, Jap. At the time, John and his four brothers and sisters were all living with Grandma Perkins on Mr. Fred Bush's place, a couple of miles from town. John's mother had already died.

"It's kinda hard to explain just how important it was for me to see my Daddy and have him with me. You see, this was the Deep South during the depression. Economic hardship and despair pretty much dominated all of life in the black community. It was a tough life, and families struggled for existence. But somehow, we endured.

"Teasing in the black community can be cruel and

66

*The Christian organizes his own emotions
and feelings and hurts
for the good of others.
Society tries to fill that void
with money, success, things,
but what it needs
is a father, a friend
and a lover.*

99

direct and strong. So if a kid doesn't have a father, he is a bastard and is open to any sort of teasing that might come his way. But I wasn't a bastard! I had a father and I knew it. My aunts and my grandmother told me so. And my father had been married to my mother. He may not have lived at home, but he was my father. He was mine! Nobody else's but mine!

"And then all of a sudden, Jap was home. My Daddy was home. He came up on a visit from Columbia, Mississippi, where he had been living, and stayed with us overnight. He arrived late one Friday night after I had fallen asleep alone in a crowded house.

"He woke me up, and I saw him in the glow of the lamp. There was love in his face. Love for me. He hugged me in his strong arms. And he talked to me. My Daddy! It was the first time someone loved me just for myself.

"It was a wonder I slept at all that night. For the joy of belonging, of being loved, was almost more than my heart could hold! And I could hardly wait for morning to proudly show off my Daddy—not my "Uncle Jap"—to all those kids who had teased me about him.

"This man was my Daddy. And I could prove it. I slept content.

"I remember the feelings more than the events of the next morning. Again Daddy talked to me, showed special love to me. I almost forgot to mind his calling me 'Baby'—what with me being the youngest. I was just happy to be with him, to see him and to touch him.

"So when he said he was going to catch a ride back to Columbia again, there was only one thing on my mind: I would go with him!

"Now you see, this was not the kind of wish where you just choose something, like vanilla instead of chocolate ice cream. It was more than a wish; it was a deep-down feel-

> **The Church is offering society
> a corporation,
> but all the while
> it's looking for
> its daddy.**

ing inside that we should, we would both go away together.

"Naturally, we would both go. No question about it. After all, he was my Daddy. Not just the man who fathered me, but my Daddy. My family!

"It was just after noontime on Saturday when Daddy started down the lane by the railroad tracks where we ran the cows. I saw he was headed toward town and started following him.

"'Daddy!'

"Jap turned and saw me following.

"'Go back. Go back.'

"The way he ordered me back sounded strange, like he was confused somewhat. Yet he really didn't sound like he was angry with me, so I followed, but at a careful distance behind.

"I wondered what was wrong. I knew my Daddy loved me. So why didn't he want me to go with him?

"As the lane ran out, Daddy moved up onto the railroad tracks. I trailed him. And when he stopped, I stopped. When he moved, I followed.

"He knew I was still there behind him, because he came back a couple of times and whupped me with a switch from a tree. After that I gauged my distance better; far enough back to run if he came toward me, but close enough to see him through my tears—and keep following him.

"I was so mixed up, I didn't know what to think. Why was Daddy punishing me? I hadn't done anything wrong. I only wanted to go with him. That's all I wanted. And I wanted it more than anything else in the world.

"Even when he switched me, I sensed that Daddy wasn't really mad at me. He just seemed worried, real worried.

"My heart was breaking. Why couldn't Daddy tell I just wanted to go with him? I was afraid, terribly afraid that, if he got out of sight, I would never see him again.

"Daddy! Please, Daddy! Take me with you. Don't leave me alone!"

"Jap stopped and looked at me once more. That strange, sad look was still on his face. I reached toward him and wanted to run to him. But I was afraid. He still held that switch in his hand. I could only stand there and cry.

"I knew that Daddy was going away without me. But I still didn't turn back. So once more he came back and whupped me a last time.

"Just then my Auntie came up. She must have missed me and followed after me. I stood there between the two of them, neither one saying anything. Then she took me by the hand and dragged me away, back down the tracks toward home.

"I looked back once, but Daddy was already gone. And with him went my newfound joy in belonging, in being loved, in being somebody for just a little while. Years would pass before I would know this joy again.

"I cried all the way back to the house, holding tightly to Auntie with one hand and carrying my heart with the other.

"What was Daddy really thinking, what was in his mind that day he left me? I never found out. I never ever really had a chance to talk with Jap in the few times I saw him again before he died.

"But I do know that, even when he punished me for following him that afternoon, he was admitting we had some sort of *relationship*. And that need for relationship was a weight I carried, a need that remained unmet for me much of the rest of my life."[1]

Fifty-three years later I walked with John down that same path. The memory is as vivid as ever. John's ministry was conceived in a lonely four-year-old heart and born in a society that longs to have a Daddy.

All of his ministry hangs on this deeply human understanding of people. Instead of being overcome by his own painful childhood, John has projected his own longings and deprivations onto the world, realizing that the loneliness he feels is the loneliness the world feels.

"The Christian organizes his own emotions and feelings and hurts for the good of others," John told me as we stood in the spot where his father had slipped away. "Society tries to fill that void with money, success, things, but what it needs is a father, a friend and lover."

And it's this profoundly human view of society that marks John's impact, not only on D'Lo, but on every community he's moved into since. "The Church is offering society a corporation," reflects John, "but all the while it's looking for its daddy."

Note
1. Portions of this episode were excerpted from John Perkins' earlier book, *Let Justice Roll Down* (Ventura, CA: GL Publications, 1976), pp. 28-31. Used by permission.

2

A Place to Make a Difference

CALIFORNIA'S Northwest Pasadena holds the dubious honor of being one of the nation's highest crime rate regions. John and Vera Mae Perkins moved there in 1981, secured a map of the area, drew a line around eight blocks and claimed that as their community.

It's become their home.

Drugs, robberies, rapes, muggings—they're the order

of the day. Fear of these realities would scare off any sensible person, but the Perkinses see a different reality: family.

"When we moved here we didn't know anybody. But now that's changed. We see kids, just 13 and 14 years old, being pulled into drugdealing and all sorts of crime. Now, we're saying, 'Hey, you can't do that to our kids! So we fight for our kids. We bought houses that belonged to the drug pushers and turned them into community centers. We're getting the pushers off the streets."

Their Pasadena ministry, the Harambee Christian Family Center, provides supplementary education, teaches practical subjects such as computer education, business development and printing and holds discipleship classes for those interested in Christianity. During the 1986 awards program of their center, five bicycles were handed out for achievement. John told his staff that one bicycle had to be awarded to a child that most needed it, and another to the meanest kid in the program. This careful attention to detail reflects the parenting heart of what John is about.

"Because this is *our* community, we own its needs," says John. Very satisfying to John is how many of the kids refer to him as "Papa" or "Grandpa" Perkins.

"The Church today is a group of people who have organized themselves together to *be Jesus* in a specific community. I don't believe in the individualistic concept that 'Jesus in me' will solve society's problems." John is vigorously committed to the gospel's focus on being a group of people in a specific place. The role of the gospel in that place is to infuse the community with the tender love of the Father in whatever form that hurting society requires. "You don't go to a community with your prepackaged gospel tracts. You teach them who Jesus is as you become a part of their lives."

In bringing this vision to the Church, John has reintroduced the term "parish." The church's parish is all the needs of the people that live within a defined geographical area. The church is not being the Church if that area doesn't begin to change and reflect the good news of Jesus.

"The New Testament Church is not the Church *everywhere,* it's the Church *somewhere.*" John says it pleases him when old-timers return to their place in Northwest Pasadena and say that it's no longer the same. He always responds, "Of course it isn't. It's not supposed to be, because now we live here." The gospel materialized when it became the visible demonstration of God's love to that region.

John's understanding of the gospel then is something very practical. It has to be "livable." Truth is that which is lived out versus that which is only thought out. Whatever I

The New Testament Church
is not the Church everywhere,
it's the Church somewhere.

can point back to and say, "There, that's what the gospel looks like," is what truth is.

This dynamic view of the gospel, as opposed to a static view, leaves John in a constant posture of learning and with the freedom to learn from just about anyone. He criticizes the evangelical church, of which he is a part, for assuming it has a corner on the truth. "It tries to protect itself, distancing itself from others, rather than living its message. If liberals don't *believe* that Scripture really makes a difference in the world today, Evangelicals don't *live* like it makes a difference in the world."

The issue of inerrancy, for example, is a nonitem when ministering in the black community. It's not a matter of good or bad, it just doesn't show up on the menu of things to be concerned about. But John won't fall into the trap of putting down people who spend a significant amount of their time preaching inerrancy. His response to them is quite simply, "Yes, I believe the Bible is inerrant, without any mistakes. Now, let's look at Amos where we read about God's demand for justice, and at 1 John 3:16-20 where we're told to love in both word and deed, or at James 2. Yes, it's inerrant. So go do it."

When you come right down to it John's a fundamentalist, and he out-fundamentals his peers. He's so secure in his relationship to God that new ideas, doctrines and institutions don't threaten him. He'll admire the devotion of Black Muslims, learn from the confessing life of a Catholic and move forward compassionately in the world with whatever new truth he has acquired, no matter what source God has used to bring it to him.

The challenge that John Perkins brings to the evangelical Christian in this regard is: "Let go of the security you gain by holding tightly to a few personalized promises and ask instead, What will the world look like if I take up my cross and follow Jesus?" Society has seduced us into thinking that life is me-centered, so we're concerned with being free of burdens. The Scriptures, however, call us to take on the yoke of Christ's burden. When Jesus told His disciples that He would no longer be in the world, He was explaining that they were to be His replacements, that they were to carry His heartache for the world and that He would live out His burden for the world through them.

"Personal religion, personal evangelism, personal salvation, personal this. The call to follow Jesus is a call to obedience, so it always begins with asking what it is that He wants."

Most Christian literature on guidance or calling, in John's view, has built into it a tendency toward disobedience. "We ask God if it's okay to do the things we're planning to do, when already the Scriptures are packed with directives." Because God is about the business of calling His people to parent society, probably the most important question to ask is simply, "Where?"

God's call on John's life was first to the poor of Mississippi. During those years he developed his theory of the three *R's*:

1. *Relocation.* Moving to a place in society where God desires to unleash His love.
2. *Reconciliation.* Being an agent of God's love in that place, so that people can be personally reconciled to their Maker and then reconciled to each other. Reconciliation on this second level includes addressing social evils such as racism.
3. *Redistribution.* Being a steward of all my goods, finances, talents and whatever else God has given me for the sake of the reconciling gospel in that place.

66

If liberals don't believe
that Scripture really makes a difference
in the world today,
Evangelicals don't live
like it makes a difference
in the world.

99

Society would want us to believe that we gain significance from our status in others' eyes. That could involve a specific role or certain possessions. Desiring significance is not wrong. It's a God-given desire that we ought to seek to fulfill. But the way we gain our significance is not in the manner society prescribes. The crowning experience of significance ought to be conversion: the awesome reality that God loves me enough to identify with me and call me His own.

The fact that I am important is already a given for I'm created in the very image of God (see Gen. 1:26). I have dignity; all of humanity has dignity. If we understand ourselves in this light, then we're free to reject society's lure to pursue things that ultimately cannot add to who we are.

Because we have eternity within us, there is the God-given desire, not only to be significant, but to *do* what is significant. "This sort of significance can only be understood in the past tense. Did it have a long term effect? Did it change anything, anyone? Significant deeds come back to the fact that they worked out, that they made a difference. The implications of what I'm doing is what makes it significant."

Significance has been reduced to praise: What do other people think of me? Am I important in their eyes? In this sense, we've twisted significance around to what is self-gratifying, to what makes me feel good. Real significant deeds however know they are worthy of praise, whether or not people give that praise.

"The person who needs cheap praise has got his identity mixed up with popularity and fame." Such a statement doesn't mean that John is against affirmation. On the contrary, he feels that when he affirms someone it is done with significance in view. His staff built an outdoor amphitheater for community activities. Rather than praising

66

*The person who needs cheap praise
has got his identity mixed up
with popularity and fame.*

99

them when it was completed, he waited until their first program was staged there. He then would pull a staff member to the side during the program and say, "It was worth all that labor, wasn't it. It was worth it."

"Most folks would want to say, 'I built this thing here,'" says John, "but we want to ask, 'Was it worth it?'"

If Christians can be freed up from society's view of significance, we'll be free to ask, "Where do I go, Lord? What do I do?"

"In God's own sovereign way, I end up feeling my life has been significant if I haven't made significance my goal. I will be able to see that my children love God and want to do His will. I will see that my neighborhood has changed and that people are believing in their own dignity and self-worth. I will see people who now have a Father and know they are really loved."

It's this Father whom John knows so personally that keeps him secure. "I've never struggled with the fact that God loves me. Deep down inside I've never doubted that reality, and that makes a difference, doesn't it?"

3

Climbing Up to the Bottom

JOHN'S UNASSUMING manner doesn't match his achievements. A third-grade dropout, he has managed to achieve a societal status that few ever know. He's written books, produced videos, founded companies, led movements of people against government policies and consequently seen changes, served on a presidential commission to inquire about the nature of hunger in the United States and received several honorary doctorates. He now serves on the board of directors of the largest Christian organizations in the United States, and just recently a movie has been released on his ministry.

And yet John Perkins is just common folk.

Traveling with him through Mississippi for a week was no exception. The first night we stayed at his son's house. Spencer is married to Nancy, a white woman from Pennsylvania and they have made John a proud fifth-time grandfather with their son. Derek, another son, was also visiting for the evening.

No sooner had John and I stepped into the house than it turned into a circus. The latest stories were being swapped simultaneously at increasing volume; hugs, kisses and admiration of the grandson managed to work their way into the pandemonium.

66

God gave me a concern for the poor.
He called me to live among the poor,
and there He gave me my understanding
of what the gospel is.

99

It was a hot, muggy July evening but that kept no spirits down. "Get me some watermelon, Spencer," John ordered. "Get me some watermelon." Turns out this is somewhat of a family ritual.

John kicked off his shoes, removed his dripping shirt and, with belly hanging unceremoniously over his belt buckle, he firmly planted his body in front of a three-foot watermelon cut lengthwise. We all joined him around the watermelon and grabbed forks that protruded from the red mass. Tales grew taller as they tried to out-tell each others' jokes, and I couldn't help but laugh as I watched Dr. John Perkins spit watermelon seeds back into the common watermelon while trying to catch a dribble that had jumped off his chin and was now scurrying down his stomach into hiding.

Laughter was mixed with watermelon and with phone calls to important names such as Chuck Colson. Somehow this was all the same John Perkins.

At one point all attention turned to a mammoth flying roach that perched itself on a beam above the table. Spencer grabbed a can of Raid while Derek readied himself on a chair. Spencer sprayed half the can's contents onto the roach, as the conversation yielded to hearsay stories that roaches are one of the few creatures likely to survive a nuclear holocaust.

Meanwhile I watched the Raid rain itself down all over our watermelon. The three men cheered for the insect's death and burst into applause when it slipped off the beam to the floor. Derek produced a butcher knife and triumphantly beheaded the enemy. Job complete, all three went back to the serious business of devouring the watermelon.

One watermelon later we had solved the question of women's rights, figured out how to turn John's children's auto business into a booming industry, solved some pro-

motional questions for three different black ministries that
had called during the commotion, watched the news,
reached agreement on South Africa and reflected on the
difference between Dr. Martin Luther King, Jr. and the
Reverend Jesse Jackson.

Before going to bed John washed out his shirt in the
kitchen sink. It's one of his nightly rituals. "I've always
wanted my children to know that a man doesn't need a lot
of shirts. But I do keep one or two good ones on hand just
in case I got to be with the big shots or attend a funeral."

John is not unaware of the status he carries in the
evangelical world. He knows that in society's terms he's a
celebrity, and he struggles with that regularly. "The most
important question for me is whether I can use that position for the good of society. Can that fact somehow help
people? My struggle is a healthy struggle. It burdens me
sometimes, but I believe it makes me a better preacher.

"I don't like how society is all polished up. I don't like

66

Let go of the security you gain
by holding tightly
to a few personalized promises
and ask instead,
What will the world look like
if I take up my cross
and follow Jesus?

99

what it's doing to people, the image it's creating. Sometimes I want to wear my pajamas to church. You know, I really think John the Baptist was right. I feel like our society needs to be confronted." John wonders if he is adjusting to society in areas where he ought to confront it. "It burdens me sometimes; it burdens me."

I accompanied John to some speaking engagements at a Christian liberal arts college. After one particularly forceful session on the need for "relocation," a starry-eyed student came up to John and exclaimed how "neat your talk was."

"Oh yeah? What did you like about it?"

The student fumbled a little and said that it was "real radical."

"Okay. So what are you going to do about it?"

John told me later, "A lot of people want to talk to a celebrity. They need to know that you don't think of yourself that way, that you really are expecting change.

"Sometimes people tell me how much they would like to 'help' me. I admit I wonder sometimes if they want to be associated with John Perkins of if they want to help me achieve my goals."

The public projects images on leaders that John finds himself fighting. "They want a celebrity. They want a confident man who looks good. The world doesn't want to see the humility that is in Christ, the brokenness that comes from Him, our weakness, our dependence."

Fanny Lou Hammer is a civil rights activist of the 1960s who left a deep impression on John's mind as to the celebrity's role. She told a group of black politicians who had finally "made it" into leadership posts that they should never allow their own importance to overshadow the people and the cause that brought them to that place. They should never allow their own interests to get in front of the

> *Every morning when I wake up*
> *and put on my suit,*
> *I have to look at myself*
> *in the mirror and ask the question,*
> *Why on earth am I here?*

cause of the people they represent. The people's interests are the leader's interests.

"She prepared me for the kind of person I want to be," reflects John.

"I have to look at the process of how I became who I am. I'm very conscious of who I am, conscious that I could pick up the phone right now and call people who would make a difference. Right now I could call the Chief of Police of Pasadena, and within minutes he would have five detectives here asking what they could do. I could do that. I realize that.

"I must see that in light of my calling. God gave me a concern for the poor. He called me to live among the poor, and there He gave me my understanding of what the gospel is. The fact that I learned about the gospel among the poor increases my commitment to them. To leave would be desertion of those who made me what I am. I would not be known in the world had it not been for the poor.

"My place of importance in life is because of the struggle of the little people, the broken people."

John concludes: "Every morning when I wake up and put on my suit, I have to look at myself in the mirror and ask the question, Why on earth am I here?" Without a doubt, the answer to that question is to bring the good news of the Father to the poor. And if John succeeds that day, he will have gone farther down society's ladder, but in his view, much closer to the heart of God.

4

Change Agent

JOHN'S ARRIVAL in this town will forever be here. He came at a painful moment in history and stood in the gap."

Leonard Smith lives on the black side of Mendenhall, Mississippi, the town to which John Perkins moved in 1960 and the town which would become the turf of some extremely painful experiences. Blacks couldn't live outside their part of the neighborhood. They couldn't vote, were largely unemployed, hungry, lived in shacks and did whatever pleased the white interests.

"John came here with the courage to make a difference. You gotta understand now that we folks were scared of change. We had been pushed down and kept down. We were afraid. But John went for it, regardless of what it took—even though his life was endangered."

What Leonard remembers most about John is that he cared. "He would stay up all night and pray with you—pray that you'd get a job, pray that your girl wouldn't get pregnant, pray that your kids would get out of the mess and go to college."

Mendenhall had seen its share of preachers who came in their fancy clothes and cars, gave a sermon, took an offering and then drove off till the next Sunday. John Perkins was different.

"John made religion practical. Preachers would say, 'You're going to hell,' if you played sports. Along comes John Perkins. He takes off his shirt and shoes and gets right in there with them. Preachers got upset with him but we didn't. He had a deep involvement with the kids and he won the hearts of the parents."

John's civil rights activities in Mendenhall have been well documented in his books. Probably one of the most surprising aspects of those days is that the blacks took their chances and got behind him.

"John's honesty and integrity were simply a matter of fact. He talked ideas a lot, and although we didn't always understand them, we liked John."

The whites tried many ways of getting rid of John— imprisonment, beatings, threats to his family—but nothing worked. He remained. In 1971, Leonard was approached by some whites with a large sum of money. "They told me to bump off John Perkins and to do it any way I liked. But to just do it."

But the lure of money to poor blacks like Leonard was no match for the power of the gospel that had taken root thanks to the faithfulness of John.

Dolphus Weary is 40 years old. In 1986, he assumed the presidency of Mendenhall Ministries—the organization that resulted from those early days of John's efforts. Dolphus became a Christian at age 17 in the tent in D'Lo next to Effie's house. He'd attended a church since age seven, but the gospel had never been clear to him until he sat under John's preaching.

Dolphus's dad left home when Dolphus was four years old. His mother and seven siblings had to fend for themselves and were helped a little by a second marriage that brought two more kids. Dolphus always felt like a second-class citizen and saw no way out of his plight.

That night in D'Lo is lodged firmly in his heart. "How can I repay the Lord for all his goodness to me?" Dolphus quotes Psalm 116:12 to summarize his years as a Christian. And he thanks the Lord for the man John Perkins who spent years discipling him, loving him and training him with a vision of what the gospel could do in Mendenhall.

"John can see something where nothing exists. He's extremely good in depressed communities. He can rise above a situation and see creative solutions." His tremendous courage, says Dolphus, gave him the ability to walk into the most negative situations and believe that something positive could result. He was *daring*, not afraid to take a chance, going against the odds, going against others.

"He would tell us," Dolphus recalls, "'Do not limit your dreams based on the resources at your disposal. Dream far beyond what you have.'"

John's effect on Dolphus's ability to pull out of his deep despair was significant, but more significant was his role model as a Christian. "You could never separate his beliefs from his life-style. He was honest with his kids about the vacuum in his own life for a father model. He was always warm with them. John would be up with his kids and us every morning at 5 A.M. We'd study the Bible together, pray and sing hymns."

Dolphus had the opportunity to leave Mendenhall and pursue a secure future, but John convinced him to stay and be a part of John's vision for what God could do there.

In those early years, they established numerous Bible studies and discipleship groups, tutored kids, did radio broadcasts on five stations, began a food program for the undernourished, built a gym to get kids off the streets, built a clinic because, according to Dolphus, their survey revealed that 85 percent of the residents had never seen a

66

*I don't like
how society is all polished up.
I don't like
what it's doing to people,
the image it's creating.
Sometimes I want
to wear my pajamas
to church.*

99

doctor (doctors would always empty the white waiting rooms before attending the black needs—no matter what the problem), began an adult education program, established a kindergarten and founded a thrift store.

John's visionary role began to stifle the ability of the 10 full-time staff to set up adequate administrative structures to keep the myriad projects running smoothly. So John decided to concentrate his efforts in Jackson, Mississippi and, in 1978, let go of Mendenhall as an independent ministry organization. In 1981, it formally incorporated as Mendenhall Ministries. Dolphus served as director under the new president.

"It's always difficult for the father to release responsibility to the son," recalls Dolphus, "and it's always difficult for the son to question the father." But Mendenhall Ministries has moved forward. It has shifted its emphasis a little to reflect the need to raise a generation of Christian leaders, although "everything we're doing is reflective of John's dream of wholistic ministry."

Mendenhall has expanded its school through sixth grade, purchased 120 acres for a farming ministry, started a legal services organization and increased its staff to 50 people.

Dolphus seems to have inherited some of John's visionary heart. He dreams that Mendenhall Ministries will become a nationwide example of a workable model for community development. He sees the need to eventually create a Christian construction company, housing project, counseling center and to establish an economic development company that will be able to employ the poor and turn money back into the community rather than into the bank accounts of the established rich people who have not used their wealth to improve the lot of Mendenhall's poor.

Currently Dolphus is working with a budget of

$850,000 and looks forward to the day when Mendenhall Ministries will be financially stable and not dependent on donations.

Artis Fletcher relinquished his presidency of Mendenhall Ministries to give more time to pastoral concerns, for the ministry also runs a church. He sees his primary role as "spiritual care."

Artis first met John when a student at a private junior high. John held Bible studies in the dorm. After completing pastoral training, planting a church, pastoring it for six years and then going for more training, Artis returned to Mendenhall in 1974 where he volunteered until becoming president.

"John shaped my early life in the Lord. More than anything else he took time with me, teaching me the basic doctrines of the Scripture, showing me how to pray, study my Bible and evangelize."

I asked Artis to describe John's strengths.

"He stands on the Scriptures and he understands them. He's a man of vision and hope. He came to a disenfranchised, despised, despairing people and showed them what could be done. He had the faith to make it happen. Not only could he see what needed to be done, but he *moved forward* to make it happen.

"It took a lot of faith in the '60s to create an oasis," Artis continues. "In the face of difficulties and hardship, faith kept going."

The ministry was very taxing on John's family during those days because the human rights confrontations brought many threats and much harassment. Pioneering and developing took long hours, demanded the total person and yet the family stayed together. "John maintained the reputation of being a good husband. There was zero scandal of being immoral, and that's amazing in the midst of a community where a lot of family unfaithfulness takes place."

Artis recalls that hardly anyone believed John could do it. Yet he pushed forward to minister in the area of felt needs. He was sure that things done close to the heart of God would be blessed by God: evangelism, discipleship, feeding the poor, standing for justice and righteousness.

"Brother and Sister Perkins started the race—and then the baton was handed onto us to continue that race. It's a race of ministry to the total person."

Like Dolphus, Artis believes the ministry was handed over at a good time. "John's a pioneer. His strengths are not in fine-tuning or operating. Before his project would reach efficiency he would move onto the next thing and endanger that project. Sometimes projects failed as a result."

Artis has learned that he needs to follow through with commitments, "even if they hurt financially." People in the community are used to dashed promises and sometimes, "John gave too many promises."

Nonetheless, John's impact on Mendenhall was "profound. He ushered in human rights; got blacks registered to vote; got blacks jobs in factories, not just fields; forced the city to give us better health care and recreation and led our community forward where we were too fearful."

John left his legacy behind in Artis just as in Dolphus. A good leader in Artis' view must be a visionary, have faith for the impossible, do everything with integrity, must love the people he serves and be committed to the task more than anyone else. Artis hopes that his future role in Mendenhall Ministries will include working to erase racial discrimination, credit problems and job problems in the community and to change legislation that negatively impacts black education.

66

*You don't go to a community
with your prepackaged gospel tracts.
You teach them who Jesus is
as you become
a part of their lives.*

99

"But for the longevity and success of our ministry I must never forget that my relationship with God is my highest personal priority, and that my leadership responsibilities should never erode the priority of my commitment to my family."

One other person in Mendenhall, C.J., demonstrates that the vision of John Perkins has made it to the third generation. C.J. started working at the Mendenhall thrift store the year Dolphus became director of the ministries. Heavily involved in the civil rights movement, C.J. had given up on Christianity because he believed the only answer was power. In 1974, he became a Christian and in 1975 moved to Mendenhall to be a part of a new church-planting effort. He met Dolphus and in 1978 signed up full-time. He is now the administrative director of Mendenhall Ministries.

"Honesty and integrity are cornerstones of our ministry. We need to *identify* community needs and then implement situations in an environment of respect and vision."

C.J. has high regard for Artis and Dolphus: "They are disciplined, trustworthy, available, honest and consistent in what they do and say." And, "I realize that how much I make financially here is not important. The question is, how long is this thing going to last—what difference will it make?"

Voice of Calvary (VOC) is the name John Perkins first used for his ministries in Mississippi. When the Mendenhall division was separated out to be an independent work, Jackson, Mississippi kept the name. In January 1982, John and Vera Mae Perkins moved to Pasadena, California and left Voice of Calvary in the hands of 29-year-old Lem Tucker as the new president.

Lem first met John at the Inter-Varsity Christian Fellowship (IVCF) mission conference, Urbana '76. He visited John in Jackson the next year and joined up with the team shortly after that. Born in Virginia, raised a middle-class black by a strong, rebellious mother, Lem says he was sent into life with a lot of fight in him.

It was only natural for John to let go of Voice of Calvary. It had outgrown him in terms of management demands. "If you build 10 bridges, one each year, it may look good at first, but 15 years down the road the first bridges will have some strong maintenance demands. VOC reached a point where it needed a strong infrastructure that could focus on the growth of current projects rather than the birthing of new ones," says Lem. "John showed his wisdom by moving on before he had to be carried away."

With a staff of 45 and several projects similar to Mendenhall Ministries, Lem is full of vision for the future. But he's very quick to give credit for his vision: "I can only see as far as I do because of the shoulders I'm standing on."

Lem wants VOC to be a replicative model for community development. "The Bible says the Church is to be the hope of the world. We ought to be the experts in human development. Everything about our work here comes under that hope."

The city of Jackson, with its population of 300,000 and 48 percent black residents, is becoming Lem's parish. More than 45 percent of the population is under 18. "We're in a desperate, urgent hour for the city. Gang life is on the increase, we're moving further away from family values, people aren't sure they can escape their world of poverty. Liberals and conservatives have failed with their one-dimensional programs. Our approach is biblically wholistic and it's the hope of the city. Ultimately we're a church—not a program."

Lem doesn't see any flash-in-the-pan answers for his

city, rather a steady, certain advance on the city with all the good news of Jesus. His favorite verse as he ponders this: "I am not ashamed of the gospel, because it is the power of God for the salvation of everyone who believes: first for the Jew, then the Gentile" (Rom. 1:16).

There are some things Lem will do differently from John. "His management sometimes had precipitous consequences. When he could have handled a staff problem with a surgeon's scalpel, sometimes he'd come busting in with a hatchet." Lem's worst memories along this line are those of getting phone calls from John as early as 4 A.M., telling him to fire someone immediately. "There was no discussion. John made a decision that to me seemed compulsive, but it was his decision to make. I delivered the bad news."

Lem admires John and believes he stands a head above his peers. "John left behind a very high percentage of black leaders in his organizations. I look at my black counterparts and see that something in them died before they got

into leadership. Not so with me; John helped me get here. He'll always be a father to me."

And on a final note: "John goes very deep into the Word. It's not a security thing or a scholarly thing. It's his life."

Thelma Anderson is 32 years old and heads up the VOC Health Clinic. Their staff of 10 helps dozens of people each day who wouldn't ordinarily get the medical attention they need. Besides taking care of the walk-in patients, the staff is asking what community dynamics need to be changed to prevent the diseases they have to treat. Malnutrition and diabetes are common problems, and the clinic hopes to make a large contribution to the overall community development.

Prices are much lower than other clinics, but they do charge just to affirm the dignity of the patients. Although patients don't know in advance, any overdue bills at the end of the year are forgiven. In 1985, they canceled over $20,000 in debts.

Thelma says the clinic communicates the message that, "You're important to us whether or not you have money, look good or smell nice." And, "We're a private physician's office, not a public clinic. This is your center, your doctor."

About John Perkins: "John is God-led. He has a clear burden for people and doesn't give up. He cares. A lot of people see wrong and oppression but do nothing about it. John submitted to the Lord's will in his life and spoke up."

Melvin, Thelma's husband, directs People's Development, Inc. (PDI), a construction company founded by John to supply affordable, good housing for the poor. Melvin was raised in D'Lo by his grandmother and started attending VOC Bible studies at age 10. "Some people disapproved of what John was doing because it wasn't ordinary, but you could almost see, feel and touch God there." John and Vera Mae were like parents to Melvin. Although not a Christian then he said he remembers praying often that God would make him a part of John's ministry one day.

At the Urbana, Illinois IVCF missions convention in 1979, Melvin said that Derek Perkins was determined to convince him to become a Christian. "Derek talked and talked and talked one night until I finally asked him just to stop talking. Derek told me that he'd either save me or bore me to death. I became a Christian that night."

After working at the YMCA for six years, Melvin became the director of PDI in 1985. More than 60 houses have been made available to poor people since its founding in 1974, and PDI continues to look for good deals. "We also fix up people's homes, doing odd jobs like wheelchair ramps and weatherization. All of our labor for the elderly is donated."

Personal religion, personal evangelism, personal salvation, personal this. The call to follow Jesus is a call to obedience, so it always begins with asking what it is that He wants.

Concerning John Perkins: "He's a brother who loves the Lord, understands the calling God placed on his heart to help those who don't have. He's a leader, motivator, friend of God."

John visits the Jackson ministry regularly and Melvin really likes that. "It always does my heart good when he's here. He's the founder, tells me things look good, tells me I'm doing a great job. Pumps me up."

Melvin had ideas of upward mobility, but John ruined that for him. "If you spend a lot of time around him, you begin to change your life-style, give up things. I realized that I was wanting to store up treasures for myself—it all seems so selfish now."

Chris Rice, one of two white leaders in the Voice of Calvary ministry, directs fund-raising. He's attracted to John for reasons that affected Melvin: "There's an integrity there when you see what he could have done, positions he could have held, salary he could have taken, lifestyle he could have led."

It's this no-nonsense understanding of Christianity together with the modeling that in Chris's view sets John apart from other voices in the evangelical world. "John is calling people back to the community, to the local level, forcing us to ask ourselves what we're doing with our lives and resources."

Chris has also been influenced by John's ability to create ministries and walk away from them. He notes that a good amount of humility is needed to recognize one's own talents may not be adequate for the next stage of growth.

"We're carrying out the vision God gave John. He drew people around himself who could help him accomplish his goals, and then he left the ministry in their hands. John didn't just leave a strong second generation of leaders behind, he left his creation at their feet."

5

In the Church

JOHN DEEPLY BELIEVES in the Church. He carries a high regard for this institution that formed the basis of survival for blacks forced through the treacherous years of slavery to struggle for freedom. But his respect for the Church has not stifled his response to its life-style. "It ain't in the world today as it ought to be."

So it was only natural that John found himself fighting the Church from day one in Mississippi. His message that called Christians to serve their local communities, bringing specific changes in the social dimensions while making personal life-style adjustments, was a direct affront to black pastors who modeled a detached life-style—and one that was lived several financial notches above that of the laity.

The established clergy clearly saw John as a threat to their financial domains. Stories would spread about John's "heretical" view of Scriptures, but the laity kept coming back to hear more of him. Without a doubt, it was his ability to preach simply and in a way that mattered to the people that won over the hearts of poor blacks, even though pastors fought hard to overcome that influence.

"You cannot preach from a pulpit," says John. "You have to preach from the parish." John always made it his

goal to understand the needs of his people and then he would go to the Bible to find answers. "When I'd speak to them I'd identify their need and sorta emotionalize it for them, let them know I understood those hurts maybe even more than they did. Then I'd open my Bible and show them what Jesus wanted to do about it."

This confrontation with pastors has left him looking suspect—that maybe he doesn't see the Church as God's primary agent for reconciliation in the world. The truth is more accurately understood however with an appreciation of how loosely John holds the *form* of the Church. He wonders if Christians ought to operate at all outside of the local church, but he doesn't confine the local church to the structure that has a building, choir and hired pastor. In fact, many of those wouldn't qualify as a church in his view. "The question we have to ask ourselves is, Have we organized ourselves together to make an impact on a specific place in the world? If not, we just might not be the Church."

In 1985, John seriously considered taking on the pastorate of a local church and confining all of his activities to the title "pastor." "People would probably think I'm all right then. I'm not the big parachurch Mac coming into the community to challenge them, but just another preacher to compete with."

John even wonders if some parachurch organizations exist because people didn't want to live under the demands of a local community. Rather it was easier to set up a structure that would benefit people "way over there somewhere." He's not dogmatic enough in this view to ignore large parachurch organizations. He serves on the board of directors of World Vision, for example, and sees his primary role there as asking questions that "bring us back to the main point. How has World Vision changed the world? Has the local community—where our headquarters are—changed for the better because we're there? Have *we* changed for the better as our attempts to change society have confronted us with Christ?"

John's loosely held grip on the form of the Church was a critical component in his being able to minister in Mississippi: "The majority in that state was Baptist, and most of the younger pastors had an older pastor over him."

Rev. Snell, pastor of Mount Wade Baptist Church in Jackson, remembers John's early successes and put it this way. "There were spiritual godfathers over the pastors. They controlled you, told you everything you could or couldn't do. And then here comes John Perkins. He didn't need the godfather's money, so the godfather couldn't tell him what to do. He became his own boss. He didn't need the endorsement of superstar gorillas to survive."

The ability to handle criticisms helped. His calling was sure, so he saw those rumors and rejections as "part of the territory." He was about the church's business and just

66

*You cannot preach
from a pulpit.
You have to preach
from the parish.*

99

needed to persevere. "I think people have been willing to reject the 90 percent of my style they dislike and yet work with me because they've been attracted to my message."

Rev. Joe Jean Walker lives in Pinola, just a few miles from where John spent his first days in ministry. Joe is black, 59 years old, became a Christian May 2, 1960 and was "called to preach that July—just when Reverend Perkins moved back to Mississippi."

Joe's memories of those early days with John are very warm: "He gave me a good foundation in the Word of God. Taught me how to study the Bible, helped me to separate salvation from works." Typical of John's style, he would go into the fields where Joe was working and pick cotton with him while talking about Scripture. "No one stood by me like he did in getting my feet on the ground."

But John's message fell on hard times with Joe as it did with other pastors who saw John confront the political powers in 1965. "John should have just accepted that folks will just misuse us. We mustn't get back at them, but remember rather that vengeance belongs to the Lord."

Joe saw no grounds for political involvement, biblically speaking. "John's friendship is more important to me than our differences, but I will say he should have stuck with the Bible. John Perkins walked too deep in the devil's territory." Joe is a firm dispensationalist and believes that certain things need to be left alone for Jesus to take care of when He returns.

"John was very hard on pastors in 1965 who wouldn't get involved in the civil rights movement. I'd say he offended many of them even though they all agree a lot of people became Christians and grew under John's ministry."

Eugene Walker, Joe's brother, remembers it a little differently. "We won't forget him. His preaching and love changed both parents and kids. Our younger generation won't be the same." Eugene has 10 biological children and eight foster children. One of them was found at two days old in a trash can, and no one was ready to help. Eugene took the child in temporarily and it never left. Three kids—ages five, six and seven—were discovered in a burned-down home with no parents to be found. Eugene took them home.

"John taught us to care for those less fortunate who lived far away." So Eugene's church started sending money overseas to the "poor and distressed," set up a scholarship fund to send local children away to college and worked for unity between blacks and whites in the community. Eugene never thought of John's life as becoming too political, rather he saw more people being helped to live a normal life. "He always cared about people's needs. It showed in everything he did."

When John and Vera Mae moved to Pasadena in 1982, they stopped in at a Sunday service of Good News Church, a little black congregation pastored by Carlos Caldwell. At the end of the service, Carlos invited members in need of prayer to come forward. John immediately went to the front. "It blew my mind how humble he was. He wanted the elders to lay hands on him just like they do everybody else. He said that he was moving into the community and needed people to love him and hold him accountable."

The effect of John on Carlos's life has been substantial. "I used to be a normal black pastor—prepare a sermon, socialize, dress well, ride well, live well. People would identify me as their pastor, look up to me and fantasize— 'That's my car, my home, looking good.' But John talked about something deeper than the basic salvation I had embraced. He talked about living out the gospel through human means, seeing the needs and sharing in that. This was more than just preaching a sermon and hearing people say amen, and then no one doing anything about it. This was living it out. For the first time I saw the gospel as something you live out."

Carlos was able to identify the distinct calling of John. "He's calling people to be a part of a community. To share one's life with the needs, foregoing the normal luxuries America affords. Putting whatever resources you have into the community for the good of others. That's not normal in the black church."

Life hasn't been the same for Carlos. He is not sure of his future vocation but knows it has to be one of serving the Pasadena community. Changes have not come easily for him either. Good News church is too small to salary him; consequently, he used to make his living selling life insurance—a profession that he is very good at and that brought in thousands of dollars every month. In 1986, he felt God was telling him to let go of that income and put his energies into the community.

"I identify with the Bible character of Gideon. There he was in the winepress threshing wheat. You're supposed to do it on top of a hill so that the wind will blow away the chaff and let the wheat drop to the ground. But no, here he is in a winepress, puffing away, trying to stay clear of the enemy. Gideon is a real chicken—a coward. The Lord comes to him and says, 'Gideon my man, man of valor.'"

That's what the Lord said to Carlos. "Colonel Caldwell, you are my man of valor. There you are preaching at Good News, teaching the Word of God, but you're in the wrong place. I want you to be identified with the sinners, absorb their problems, get involved in the fight."

The command was not an easy one. Carlos saw the territory as bad enough to "scare anyone to death." But

The Church today is a group of people who have organized themselves together to be Jesus *in a specific community. I don't believe in the individualistic concept that 'Jesus in me' will solve society's problems.*

more difficult to deal with were idols that had been built in his life. Just as Gideon took his men through the land one night and tore down idols, so Carlos identified idols in his own life that would prevent him from being faithful to the call God was putting in his heart.

"Identify. That's the big one. I had money, success, big car, all the things that made me somebody. And then God said to walk off the job."

It hasn't been easy or automatic. There was no role model in Carlos's life for such a radical step, so he asked John to help him "carry out God's will."

He reflects, "It's not the sort of thing you just read about and then do. I needed to see John and Vera Mae struggle to be obedient. I needed to get close to them and understand their hurts as they gave up close friends in order to move into our community. I couldn't have done it without them."

That struggle continues for Carlos. He spent six months working full-time for John and now he's praying for the next step. Status will never be the same again, however. "I see now that I don't want to live the rest of my life just to get the position money brings."

His future calling? "God has already spoken. I believe the Bible to be true and I must do what it says. There's no prayer or meditation about it. Just do it. Jeremiah had no supernatural thunder, lightning, no earthquake. That is where I am now. Based on my convictions, I'm where God wants me to be."

Thanks to the faithfulness of John Perkins, Carlos believes his church has undergone a fundamental change. "You don't hear us talking so much about what God can do for us. We're asking the question now what God wants to do through us."

John loves the Church and the testimony of people like

Carlos who are struggling to steer their churches back into the community. Seeing churches move in the direction God intended gives him energy to face the challenges of the next day.

6

With the Rich

ANYONE DIRECTING a ministry that depends on financial donations no doubt faces the question, How do people with a lot of money fit into my fiscal solution?

John has struggled some with this concern and over time has concluded that people who are well-off financially should be treated no differently than those without. He's concerned that he could water down his message with the view of attracting their dollars, and that would, in his mind, be to forsake his calling.

"I've never expected to receive a million-dollar gift. If I ever do, I'd better look closely at my message and wonder where I've slipped." A certain freedom comes with this mind-set and a couple of good friendships with people who steward millions of dollars have resulted.

Howard Ahmanson oversees a million dollar charitable trust. He's just 35 years old and has been a friend of John's for five years. "John has the ability to inspire and create community," says Howard. "He's obviously a leader among blacks. He's a model to them, showing them how to live their lives without depending on the state. As far as the whites are concerned, he's given us freedom. Freedom to serve and work toward reconciliation without the feeling of guilt."

I'm not very good at asking
rich people for money.
But I can share
my life with them,
and that includes
my understanding of the good news.
I just pray
they will be better off
for having met me.

Howard feels that whites have been manipulated by guilt for the last couple of decades and sees John as one of the first to rise above that kind of motivation. Consequently, John gets a hearing from people like Howard.

"Two kinds of people seem to hang around John," relates Howard, "the radical left—because they like a man who is black and talks about justice, and the so-called reconstructionist right—because they like what John has to say about state subsidies not being the salvation of the poor." Howard, coming from the right, has been influenced by John. They've traveled together through poverty zones in the United States as well as in India and Australia.

"John's three *R*'s have a frightening sound to them. When he talks of redistribution he is not necessarily talking of assets—mainly skills. If we redistribute assets right off, it will be like people who get the lottery ticket. A year later they're worse off, because of the financial hypoglycemia that happens when you drop a large sum of money in someone's lap. Relocation is a scary one. Ghettos have gotten worse when the middle-class blacks moved out. I certainly don't want to go back to the old Jim Crow days, but Harlem isn't a place for everyone."

Howard, who lives in Orange County, California, has been influenced by John to take on the county legally for planning to rezone parts of the county. "They're going to relocate 25,000 poor people with the introduction of one simple zone law. They don't want certain people living there, so they push up the standard of life, chase out the needy and replace them with steel and glass and fancy buildings."

In what may seem like a rather unusual statement for the Reconstructionist: "The rich are using the power of the state to oppress the poor."

Howard says that John has convinced him God has a special concern for the poor. "I don't think He automatically favors them, but He does have a special concern for them because we have a special *unconcern* for them."

The main message of John, as Howard sees it, is that Christians have to be concerned about structural evil. "Whites have to be burdened about structural evil, if they want to be well-rounded Christians. We have to begin with intercession and see where that leads. For me, it began with redevelopment bonds. I won't buy them. And then the message to blacks is, 'Don't use structural evil as an excuse for your poverty!' In a way, his message is a two-edged sword."

Roland Hinz owns a magazine publishing company that publishes six dirt bike-type monthlies. Born and raised in Germany, he remembers the postwar years as if they were today. "I still eat all the food on my plate. There was a lot of starvation and suffering those days." Four years ago he met John Perkins at a meeting in Pasadena's Lake Avenue Congregational Church. John's sensitivity to poverty attracted Roland to meet this man who had decided to make a difference in Northwest Pasadena. Roland says his life has been changed dramatically by John.

"When John the Baptist was in prison he sent two disciples to Jesus to check up on Him. This is what Jesus told them to tell John: 'The lame walk, the blind can see and the gospel is being preached to the poor.' The conservative churches have shied away from social action and concentrated only on spiritual problems. But I'm convinced now after studying the Old and New Testaments that we have a genuine obligation to the whole thing. The thing that really got the Bible's prophets upset was the way Israel treated the poor and the widows—social injustice. The apostle John tells us that true, undefiled Christianity is

*Whites need to realize
that the blacks,
who are mostly poor,
tend to accommodate themselves
to the rich.
They think that will help them
move out of their poverty.*

reflected in how we treat the widows and orphans. I buy that."

If there's anything he wants to contribute his life toward, Roland says, it is the poor. His church is currently going through a $17 million building program. "Unless this gets us directly involved in ministry to the poor then we will have missed the boat."

Although Roland cautiously underlines that he is not a bigot, he says that John has given him a new outlook on blacks and their special needs. "John identifies with them. That's a whole new thing for me. It's not a matter of just throwing money at people. The bottom line is addressing the real needs of people. He calls it 'wholistic' and I've become sensitive to that."

Roland feels, along with Howard, that John is the first black he has met who has not politicized the issue of poverty. He's called for true identification with the poor while at the same time pointing to the need for the poor to lay aside prejudices that put smoke screens in the way of their seeing some of their own problems.

"John's big enough to use unpopular solutions to problems, if he senses they're the best. He called in several police to help with heavy-weight drug pushers. Some people in his position would not be able to accept that police are legitimately concerned with dope problems." The poor, and especially poor blacks, have had so many negative encounters with the law that the police have become a symbol of oppression to them.

Roland serves as treasurer on John's Board of Directors. He spends at least a half a day each week with the ministry and often much more. At times he has spent as much as 20 hours per week while setting up a special banquet or hosting an outside speaker.

"John is a real friend. I believe he really appreciates

> *There is no biblical idea*
> *that God ever gives us ownership*
> *of the earth or its resources.*
> *The earth is always 'the Lord's,*
> *and the fulness thereof.'*
> *Christians are called*
> *only to be stewards*
> *of His resources.*

me. He called me up on Christmas morning to tell me I'm the first brother he's calling and to say how much he appreciates me. He does that on a consistent basis. I had a heart attack a couple weeks ago. I called him to ask for prayer, and I know he's praying for me now. That makes you want to stand up next to him."

Roland's future vision for Pasadena calls back John's work in Mississippi. "We need to find specific people now whom we can disciple with John's vision. Jesus got His disciples together and poured a great deal of energy into them. That's what we need to be doing here."

It's clear that John has wiggled his way into Roland's heart and given him a vision for his parish in Northwest Pasadena. "I'm not very good at asking rich people for money," says John. "But I can share my life with them, and that includes my understanding of the good news. I just pray they will be better off for having met me."

Howard and Roland would answer in the affirmative.

7

Renegade

JOHN GREW UP picking cotton for white farmers. The little home he lived in was owned by the farmers and, in the true sense of the term, he was a slave. Economic and legal barriers made it nearly impossible to live much differently. Many black families simply tried to cope. Others steadily worked toward a vision of independence. The Perkins family had a different approach.

Many of the Perkinses quite simply majored in crime—became outlaws. As best they could tell, crime was the quickest way to success, so whatever worked was game. Most of the family were risk-takers, immoral and corrupt, and were known by some as the "sin company."

Stealing cars and selling the parts, gambling, bootlegging liquor and shooting nasty competition all added up to a normal day for them. John's Uncle Bill Perkins was particularly mean and nasty, and John can remember admiring his uncle's iron will and intestinal fortitude. He was always on the run from the police, and John recalls the day when the police finally caught up with Bill at home. He hid in the bush while police searched the house and surroundings.

Finally, the frustrated police shouted to John's

66

America is a racist institution
and is looking for ways
to justify that
rather than confessing it.

99

grandma that, if she saw Bill, she should tell him that they would shoot him dead on the spot, no questions asked. Uncle Bill couldn't bear to stay quiet while hearing all this and shouted back through the bush that he'd rather die than go to jail—there was too much cotton to be picked in the fields to be sitting in jail. And he told the police that anyway they didn't have enough guts to shoot him.

They didn't catch Uncle Bill that day but they did one Sunday. John remembers seeing the gun pointed at the head of his handcuffed uncle and thinking the end had finally come, but the next thing he knew there was a scuffle, and Uncle Bill had managed to run off free behind some buildings. A couple of years later, however, life caught up with Bill—he died in prison.

Unknown to their plantation owner, John's Aunt Lillie Mae turned the whole slave quarters into a thriving casino. She was careful to do her work well, cook the master's food just right and never give a hint of impropriety. John was often sent to white homes to do chores to please whites and to show a certain air of industry should any questions arise regarding the money at their disposal.

The Perkins name was a bad one among peers and John experienced redemption for it at the same time he was saved. He rarely introduces himself as John—it's always John *Perkins*. He feels genuinely thankful every time he hears it and in a spiritual sense is very proud of it. Few things are more gratifying to him than listening to his children introduce themselves as kids of John Perkins. Not John or Dr. Perkins, but John Perkins. It's all good to him, totally redeemed.

Redeemed though his name became, it took a while for his own redemption to smooth out some of John's plantation behavior. The fighter in him never allowed him to accommodate himself to white demands. When confronted with the powerful, oppressive system of the South and the hardship that it brought to bear on the blacks, he simply shifted into a scheming mode and sought the best approach to secure equal rights.

During one election campaign in Mendenhall the word got out that blacks were going to be barred from the election booths. John had put weeks into voter registration drives, and he decided that defeat was not an option. Two nights before the election day he held a rally in the local black church. After getting the people all worked up about the election and the fact that whites were trying to bar them, he popped the question, "How many of you own guns?"

Dozens of hands went up and John directed that the next day they were to go to the city hall at equal intervals and register their guns. After that they were to go to the ammunition store and buy enough rounds "for a regular war." Word spread quickly that next day that it looked as though the blacks were "fixin' for something big," while the black women "confided" in their white home employers that the black men seemed to have reached the limit of their patience over not being able to vote.

On voting day the booths were open to everyone.

John's kids remember a few incidents during the civil rights struggle where his anger pushed him to dangerous limits: Some white youths drove back and forth in front of his house one day shouting all sorts of insults. John finally went out to the yard and told them to leave and never come back, "if they knew what was good for them." The youth had never been spoken to in this way and black jaws dropped as the car drove off. Minutes later it returned, however, drove onto the lawn and began to spin its wheels, tearing up the turf. John ran outside screaming threats and they laughed at him while driving off shooting a

> *I don't begin with the question,*
> *Is it lawful?*
> *Rather, I begin with the question,*
> *Is this a good thing to do?*
> *It may be legal, it may not.*
> *The law is not the final word.*

gun into the air. Incensed at the humiliation, he grabbed his gun and drove after them, firing many shots at the car before it was out of firing range.

Not your normal behavior for a minister of the gospel.

It wasn't John's normal behavior either that at times he couldn't control the rage that stirred inside him; rage stirred by his hatred for this oppressive system under which they all lived and by the memories of holding his dying brother in his arms as his life slipped away—fatally shot by white police shortly after returning home from military service.

The reality of John's relationship today with people like Howard and Roland is nothing less than a miracle. Those closest to him in the early days say that he hated whites and believed that he had nothing to contribute to their salvation.

Desperation, hopelessness, powerlessness, humiliation. They all contributed to the renegade who today still empathizes with terrorists—not because he agrees with their deeds, but because he understands their plight.

"Had I not become a Christian and been restrained by my understanding of God revealed in Jesus, I would have gone that way. I was almost there. They feel hopeless and they've had to ask what might be the appropriate action to express that hopelessness. Nobody is listening to them, nobody is willing to understand their needs. When I read it in the paper I say, 'Oh, that's terrible,' but I understand."

John remembers sitting in a room with other blacks plotting means to change the system. Terrorist options would always surface eventually. As tempting as they may have been, he always managed to turn them down.

John, however, did initiate an attempt to hurt the financial strength of the state and federal governments. "If they had no money, they couldn't control us." He orga-

nized a clandestine, statewide drive to get all blacks on welfare and qualified for food stamps—a movement that he figured might sweep the whole nation. It didn't succeed but, at the time, it "seemed a lot more reasonable than blowing up bridges and buildings."

John's experience in the Brandon, Mississippi jail where he was horribly beaten within a hair's breadth of death changed a lot in him that will be discussed later. It did bring him face to face with the methods he was using to confront evil, and through that painful process he concluded that the reconciling power of the cross was the only force capable of bringing total change.

"I began to see the sickness of hatred and racism. I began to realize that those people were being controlled by something very ugly that was dehumanizing them."

The renegade in John is not gone, it has been reined. This hasn't affected his view of racism and he still crusades forcefully against it.

In 1986 he was a keynote speaker at a national reconstructionist conference. Just before John spoke, a white South African had the podium. He said that South Africa does not have a problem with racism, it has a problem with the American media which projects the wrong image to the American public.

"So the big problem is American media! When I got up to speak I told the conference that I couldn't speak before responding to the earlier message. I said I felt sorry for him because I lived through the same blind spot in our nation and heard the same music in Mississippi. I said I felt sorry for him that he said the blacks have rights which need to be respected and that things like sanctions were just muddying the real issue. I told him that until whites honestly accepted that blacks should have equal rights with them to talk about anything else is pure garbage."

John hasn't let up on racism in the United States either. "America is a racist institution and is looking for ways to justify that rather than confessing it."

Although, in his mind, there are exceptions to the rule, John sees the whole church growth movement— particularly the "homogenous unit" principle—as one way racism is being sanctified. Whites move away from neighborhoods that turn black, white churches relocate to white areas and the gospel's call to be reconciled to each other is simply ignored.

"Whites need to realize," says John, "that the blacks, who are mostly poor, tend to accommodate themselves to the rich. They think that will help them move out of their poverty. In *Roots* you have the fiddler, Phil, who always fiddled for the white folks. Whites liked to see their poor blacks laugh—happy. When Phil was about to die he said he wouldn't fiddle anymore—wasn't going to make white folks think he was happy."

John is seen as a renegade for continuing to stir the pot, but he's convinced whites actually believe blacks are doing okay and are basically happy with their lot.

"We have to give blacks the courage to tell the truth to whites, to stop accommodating themselves to white demands, to believe they have dignity. And we have to tell whites they're still racist."

John would still be considered a renegade by many where the law is concerned. In his years in Mississippi he came to see the law as an institution created by the powerful who wanted to protect their interests. It's more than that of course; he acknowledges society has good laws which are beneficial for all well-meaning citizens.

"I lived as a black man in an oppressed society. I've always been working for the progress of that oppressed people in the context of a white government system. That

> *Because people had gotten used
> to measuring their lives
> by external laws,
> Jesus regularly had to remind them
> that love fulfilled
> all the requirements
> of the law.
> They killed
> that Renegade.*

system was not created to give liberty and justice to blacks, so basically everything I was doing in Mississippi was in violation of the law. Most white folk would have accused me of being a person of no integrity. Their standards had become the measure of what is ethical, rather than the Scripture's call for justice being what is ethical."

Whites become accustomed to thinking of the law as good because that's their basic experience of it. It was created for them. When something needs to be done that is outside the parameters of the law, whites are used to having the power to adjust those laws to fit their interests. The blacks' experience on the other hand is that laws rarely ever change so that they actually benefit. "So I don't begin with the question, Is it lawful? Rather I begin with the question, Is this a good thing to do? It may be legal, it may not. The law is not the final word."

Conservative churches in the States have recently shown their freedom along this line as the law relates to abortion. Discussions have regularly surfaced posing the question, "What would you do if the government required you to abort after your second child?" The answer is, "Break the law, of course." The freedom that John experiences now is less defined than the "big abortion question" and leaves a good number of people viewing him as abusing God's system of law and order.

John reflects on the persecution Jesus encountered for breaking laws instituted by the Pharisees. "Because people had gotten used to measuring their lives by external laws, Jesus regularly had to remind them that love fulfilled all the requirements of the law."

And with a glint in John's eye, "They killed that Renegade."

8

Spirituality

SEPARATING THE SPIRITUAL from the earthly does not come very naturally for John. For people who spend significant amounts of time around him, the common experience is that he is in constant conversation with God and in constant conversation with the world.

"Spirituality begins with taking a step toward God. You realize your own sin, confess it and then begin a daily walk with Jesus on the earth."

For John that daily walk is both an eternal reality and a very physical reality. Spirituality only makes sense when it involves both God and the human race. "Spirituality is like breathing: inhaling is taking in the presence of God, exhaling is interacting with the world. It's like walking; being constantly aware of God—the one foot, and constantly aware of people—the other foot.

"I don't approach things spiritually before I approach them naturally. I believe the spiritual is supposed to make the natural better. We are earthly creatures, so if there's a spiritual reality it should work itself out in the natural dimension." Eternal life in John's view begins at salvation. Because it begins on earth it isn't simply a spiritual transaction.

Spirituality should also make us highly conscious of our sin. The degree to which we live out our earthly calling will determine the degree to which we understand just how dirty we are. The more we're involved with the world the more we'll understand that spirituality is a life of confession. The beauty of this understanding of spirituality is that "it underlies both my importance as a child of God—being accepted by Him as dirty as I am, and my humility as His servant—realizing that it's only by His grace that I'm allowed to serve.

"Being spiritual will also mean that I'm constantly aware of the impact I have on other people. When I walk into a room I say to myself, 'John, you are affecting everyone in this room eternally, because you're an eternal person.' It motivates me to have a positive impact in any environment I find myself."

John's view of spirituality was greatly influenced when working in Kenya in 1980. He lived with people who had a very low standard of existence, but a very high level of spirituality. "Their quality of life was higher than mine. They had a personal love for Jesus Christ and they always talked about Him as if He were sitting there right with us."

Reading the Bible, figuring out its earthly application while speaking to Jesus about the content has become a daily routine of John's. It's not a discipline or ritual, it's what his life is. The daily tasks around the Center when he's not traveling—like pulling weeds, sweeping the premises, washing the dishes and the car or scrubbing the kitchen floor—are times of praying with his hands. If you approach him at those moments, he draws you into his prayers, involving you with the thoughts on his heart.

"Spirituality also means contentment. I feel we've lost that in our rich society. We aren't grateful when we sit down to the table and eat. That ought to be a highly spiri-

*Spirituality begins
with taking a step
toward God.
You realize
your own sin,
confess it
and then begin
a daily walk
with Jesus on the earth.*

tual reality—our Father in heaven supplied us with another meal to continue our service to Him.

"When I grew up we didn't have a fridge. It still amazes me that I can go to my fridge now, open it up, choose a drink and put ice in it. We never had ice. Cold water is a blessing. Food that's immediately available is a blessing. I hope I never lose the sense of that touch of God.

"A person who is always craving more, caught up in material-pursuits is not in touch with the spiritual. Satisfaction is spirituality."

John wants his ministry to constantly be in a state of vulnerability where they're in a position of seeing God as the only answer. He fears that the Church has become captive to the "almighty dollar" and will not do anything that could jeopardize income. The economic system of the world—the basis for determining goals and plans—has become the system of the Church. After 25 years of full-time ministry, John and Vera Mae still live from week to week, wondering how God will supply the next dollar to meet the needs of the ministry.

"Money is the answer to very few of life's problems. We've been fooled into thinking it is the answer to everything, and we plan accordingly.

"The American dream has trained us to think that personal happiness and our individual pursuits are important. Prosperity is all a part of that. And then we are left with guilt that is unresolved because we're holding onto a life that we shouldn't even be pursuing. The Lord has planned something much better for us, and He convicts us, but we hold on because society and the Church have told us to. So then we build these big counseling programs to help us manage our guilt, to help us order our lives around our unspiritual decisions."

"The Church has lost its ability to help Christians deal

Spirituality is like breathing:
inhaling is taking in
the presence of God,
exhaling is
interacting with the world.
It's like walking:
being constantly aware of God—
the one foot,
and constantly aware of people—
the other foot.

Spirituality also means contentment.
I feel we've lost that in our rich society.
We aren't grateful
when we sit down to the table and eat.
That ought to be a highly spiritual reality—
our Father in heaven supplied us with another meal
to continue our service to Him.
I hope I never lose the sense
of that touch of God.

with guilt and sin. Guilt should be viewed as a gift.

"The source of guilt is sin. If we accept that, we're on the road to spirituality. The Bible says if your conscience condemns you, there's something wrong. Guilt is like getting close to a fire—you can feel the heat. It's a safety valve. Or think of it like fever in the body. Be careful, you may have an infection somewhere. Accept it as a sign."

The Roman Catholic church has used the confessional as an effective way for people to acknowledge their guilt and confess it. Evangelicals have overreacted to that practice, privatized their sin and condemned the Catholics for charging people to deal with their sins. "All we've done instead is sent people to professional therapy. They pay $60.00 an hour, which is much more than they'd pay at a confessional, and they still go away not admitting their sin."

Just as John preaches from people's problems, his personal problems become a springboard to spirituality. "I go to the Bible whenever I go through a personal crisis. The Scriptures are capable of leading me into all wisdom." Most of John's personal problems, in his view, are the result of poor decisions—in other words, he's brought them on himself. "Wisdom, walking close to God, is in part the ability to make good decisions. As I reflect on my problems I usually have to conclude that I got myself there."

Much of John's life is filled with problems related directly to his ministry. "My life is wrapped up in my calling, so I can hardly call those problems personal. They are what comes with being at war with the world. If I don't find myself wrestling with those kinds of problems, then it's an indicator that somewhere along the line I stopped doing battle."

If truth is what we are able to live out as Christians,

rather than a set of intellectually derived doctrines, then spirituality is the life that makes that truth live. It's meaningless apart from the living; it's the only meaning to living. And in John's view it's the only door to intimacy with Christ.

"'Apart from me, you can do nothing,' Jesus said. That's truth in motion, that's spirituality in motion. There's something very freeing about waking up in the morning, laying it all at Jesus' feet. And there's something very satisfying about laying your head down at night knowing you've lived in the heavenlies all day and that the earth is a better place for it."

9

Afflictions of Discipline

SOME PEOPLE just live. I understand my living. I'm not ashamed of my upbringing. I've taken advantage of the virtues that could be developed in my hostile environment. Some people get lost because they don't know how to."

Pain. It's been a central part of John's life from birth. Fortunately for him, by God's grace he's been able to grow by it rather than be crushed. Some pain was the result of being black in the Deep South, other pain came about from his own failures and a good amount of pain must be described as "God only knows why.

"Maybe we ought to accept pain as the by-product of what God is doing in us. Maybe God knows that pain is a necessary part of the process that brings out the beauty and warmth in us that will benefit society. In the end, we ought not to curse suffering because that could be God's option for discipline."

When John reflects on his upbringing: growing up without a mother or father, a "heathen" environment with little

moral training, he thinks his suffering has been one of God's ways to work into him the beauty of Christ that his childhood never offered.

It's clear that John has used his painful, lonely childhood as a bridge to understand and love the world's oppressed. And in other ways pain has been at work in his life. Probably the most dramatic and least talked-about experience is his beating in the Brandon jail during 1970. John had been arrested and jailed several times before February 1970, but this time the police had some particularly savage intentions for John. They ambushed him on a highway one evening after a march in Mendenhall, arrested him and then took him to a jail cell where they systematically beat him senseless. John recalls the horror of being smashed to the ground, kicked in the head, stomach, groin and legs until he could no longer feel anything.

After a while the police would return and repeat the whole process, joking and telling John that his death would be sure but that it would be real slow. Several times he slipped into unconsciousness, only to go through the same sickening routine when he came to. At times they would shove some papers in his face and shout at him to read. Struggling to open his mouth that was bloodied, trying to see through eyes that were all but swollen shut, John heard them express their anger and impatience at "this nigger who can't read." They drank heavily and in a state of drunken stupor they forced a bent fork deep into his throat and way up his nose.

With the help of the civic league of that county, Vera Mae was able to secure John's release before they killed him. By that time his head had a bump the size of a baseball, filled with blood. The special care of a doctor over a few weeks finally brought John back into stable condition.

The experience had a profound effect on his life.

"My world came to an end and I accepted it. I knew that I had to find a new way of ministry, a new way of living my life, but I didn't know if I would go on. Life stood still for me and I felt like I had died inside. I concluded that my life had no meaning, no significance to add to society. I knew that I was a Christian but couldn't see what good that meant."

Eventually John recovered enough emotionally and physically to face the suffering he had experienced. "I was confronted with the sickness of hatred and racism and realized that I had not been living my life with love for the white man. It became a deep time of repentance for me when I was confronted with my own sin. *I* was a sinner and my sin was big—bigger than that of my oppressors. I encountered the love and forgiveness of Jesus in a whole new dimension and for the first time began to love whites."

John looks back now and can say that pain was good for

*Maybe we ought to accept pain
as the by-product of what God
is doing in us.
Maybe God knows that pain
is a necessary part of the process
that brings out the beauty
and warmth in us
that will benefit society.
In the end, we ought not
to curse suffering
because that could be
God's option for discipline.*

him. Somehow in God's sovereign way he was being told that he was loved and that he should love others. The *power* of God's love became so evident to him that his evangelistic efforts became more effective—he could testify to the miracle of God working through bitterness and hatred.

This Brandon jail hardship has set John apart from others who lead similar movements in that his driving force today not only comes from an understanding of the biblical call for justice, but also from an agonizing encounter with the dehumanizing ploys of Satan. Whites who suffer from racism need to experience Christ's forgiveness, need to see that the only enemy is Satan, just as John had to learn at the hands of his abusers in that jail cell. "If you forgive them," John could hear Jesus saying, "I'll forgive you."

Many times civil rights movements have been led by people who are more committed to corporate justice than they are to the ministry of biblical reconciliation. John began to lead a movement that day which said, "Forgiveness must penetrate all our relationships." Although that lesson took some time to work its way into a ministry that had already filled its ranks with idealistic angry people, both black and white, John was able to move Voice of Calvary to a point where that soothing love of Christ became the ministry's hallmark.

The physical torture that John's body went through in that Brandon jail, the emotional toll in many ways, coming back to life and accepting the deeper love of Christ for himself and the oppressors wreaked havoc on his body. Two years later John had a heart attack and underwent some radical abdominal surgery that included the removal of 2/3 of his stomach. How much was from the beatings, how much from the emotional strain, is unclear, but John has not been free of physical pain for the last 16 years. At nights he sleeps no more than four hours because the pain becomes too much to handle.

"Many times I have to get up at 3 or 4 A.M. and begin my day's work. I've had to adjust my life to accommodate this pain and have learned to live with less sleep."

The nation's best medical practitioners and charismatic healers have not been able to relieve the pain. John stopped asking God why a long time ago and began asking Him to use it as a channel for loving the world. He believes that it has kept him humble, dependent and empathetic of others. "I know it's by God's grace that I live each day, and when someone tells me how much they're hurting I can say, 'I know what you mean.'"

Harold "H." Spees worked very closely with John from 1973 to 1984. He currently serves on his foundation's board of directors. H. remembers some of John's pain in dealing with whites and, being white himself, suffered from the anger that occasionally flared up in John. They have an unusually close relationship from having worked through the battle zone together over several years, and will still call each other long distance regularly at three or four in the morning.

That relationship nearly broke off at an early stage when H. first joined John. Confronting John with some of his negative attitudes resulted in John's giving H. immediate notice. "I don't need you any more. Just pack up your bags and move along today."

H. knew that the confrontation was racially based and had the maturity to stick it out rather than be insulted. He went inside the community house, thought for a little while and then returned to John with the news that he wouldn't leave until God told him to leave. And H. added, "If you don't like that then maybe *you* should move along!" That embarked them on a road together that led to many frank,

> *I was confronted*
with the sickness of hatred and racism
and realized that I
had not been living my life
with love for the white man.
It became a deep time
of repentance for me
when I was confronted
with my own sin.
I was a sinner
and my own sin was big—
bigger than that
of my oppressors.

heated discussions, often leaving office workers in tears, but it's put two people together who are now closer than brothers.

H. remembers a sermon John gave one Sunday in Jackson, Mississippi just after a white medical doctor resigned over a dispute. "Some of it was John's fault, but he didn't see it that way. In the middle of his sermon all this anger surfaced and he said, 'I don't know if white folks and black folks can ever be reconciled.' He went on to name me and said that I'd probably leave the community when my kids were old enough to marry—that I'd move somewhere far away from blacks so none of my kids would marry one. That struck my heart like a hot sword. Like a knife it stuck into my heart."

Embarrassed and ashamed for John, H. slipped out of the church and walked home, crying all the way. He threw himself on his bed and sobbed until he became angry. He jumped in his car, drove back to the church to confront John, only to discover that he had left for the airport already.

"I raced to the airport and found him in the boarding area with 10 minutes before the boarding. I cried out loud in front of all those people. I told him, 'You have no right in the world to say that to me. How can you let bitterness go so far?' People were staring at us—me screaming, with tears streaming down my face, and John looking like a beat puppy!"

The two men were able to reconcile there, and John stepped on the plane a somber, humble person, having to gear up for his next motivational talk.

One of John's disciplines has been learning to live with the shortcomings that are natural with his giftings. He has been good at giving over ministries into the hands of people who have the wills necessary to go the next mile—but

those transitions have not always been healthy.

John founded an impressive Thrift Store Company just before resigning as president of Voice of Calvary. The decision had not been carefully made and the project became a financial burden of a little less than $100,000. People had counseled John to avoid the idea, but he was sure it was a good concept.

Moving away from Jackson, he left the store under the management of his son and the control of the new president, Lem Tucker. John promised Lem that he would raise funds for the Thrift Store along with his new responsibilities, but he never came through with that commitment—partially because the board of directors felt the financial pressure would be a good motivation for the new directors to implement sound business goals.

John began to lose sight of the fact that this failure was his own doing. His son Spencer was doing a miserable job—yet the best that could be done under the circumstances—and Lem was putting in 100-hour weeks trying to work into his new position as president. John began to say the guys didn't have the "guts to hang in there and do a good job." H. took leadership and called John to fly back to Mississippi and resolve the problem.

"We just went down point-by-point, reminding him of the decisions he had made, critical decisions that had doomed the project to failure. We pointed out all the judgments he had made, the people he had hurt with his comments and the legacy of empty promises left behind. We made it powerfully clear, though not in anger, that he had messed up, blamed the people victimized by his own doing and put his ego in front of his son's needs. That made a visible impact on him, but nothing too spectacular."

John was staying in the home of a dentist who was out of town, and H. remembers the phone call he received from John the next morning. "He was weeping and said, 'I don't think that I can go on.' It scared me because I thought I was hearing a drastic message. He just said it over and over, and I began to fear for his life." H. handed the phone to his wife and instructed her to keep talking, raced over to the house on the gravel roads as fast as he could stay in control of his car, and there he found John laying on the floor, "wallowing and broken."

"I have never seen anybody more broken, more weeping. We prayed and prayed, and eventually he had the grace to see that God had not forsaken him, but that He knew John's future and frailties. We saw how good God is."

That deep humility and the ability to make responsible decisions when confronted with weaknesses has made H. an ever-loyal, committed follower of John.

From these trying times that tend to cut right into the soul, John has learned that retreat into the presence of God is the best solution. It's not uncommon for him now to grab his Bible and go to bed when these sorts of pressures hit. He'll sleep, pray, read his Bible, pray, sleep, read and so on until he feels that God has given clarity, his joy is restored and his strength is regained to move forward.

He has also learned from these hardships that God can move him out of the picture at any moment. He accepts that death is a likely possibility given his physical state, and he always carries his resignation letter with him to ensure that he's not clinging to something God wants him to turn loose.

"That can be a scary thing," recalls H. "I remember when we had just bought a $15,000 x-ray machine for our new medical clinic. A large townwide dedication service was planned and we were all excited at how this was a symbol of God's supply and blessing to our ministry."

> *Society exalts people,*
> *but it's not the same*
> *as God's exalting.*
> *A girl crowned 'Miss America'*
> *is exalted and given a name*
> *that carries public honor with it.*
> *She herself is no different.*
> *But I'm* John Perkins.
> *I've been redeemed.*
> *I have been lifted up*
> *into the loving care of the Father,*
> *and now my name has new meaning.*
> *It carries the scars of my life*
> *and the salvation of my Lord.*

The night before the service a heavy rainstorm hit the town and flooded the black side of town, leaving some houses adrift. The x-ray machine was totally demolished and the spirits of all quite dampened.

"It depressed John so much. He began to talk about it being time to resign, needing to move on to New Jersey to accept a pastorate." H. had no doubt John could easily walk away, the question was: Would John only do so when God told him to?"

Fortunately John saw his itchy feet as a response to his depression and kept leading the Voice of Calvary ministries. Before long he was able to see the x-ray machine replaced and an exciting dedication ensued.

Some other pains in John's life that could have become occasions for bitterness and barriers to progress have instead become opportunities to trust God for His saving grace to shape him and use him.

"As far back as I can remember, my life has been a life of pain. My mother died, I grew up without a father, lived in a house of poverty, underwent ridicule constantly, carried the stigma of my uncles who were bad, degenerate people and lived in hatred for people who did things like kill my brother just because he was black. When God saves us, he exalts us. He takes all the pain and muck of our past and miraculously turns it into something glorious.

"Society exalts people, but it's not the same as God's exalting. When a girl is crowned 'Miss America' she is exalted in the public's view because she has been given a name that carries public honor with it. She herself is no different. But I'm *John Perkins*. I've been redeemed. I have been lifted from my sorrows into the loving care of the Father, and now my name has new meaning. It carries the scars of my life and the salvation of my Lord.

"You may think it's arrogant for me to say I like seeing

my name on my letterhead. When I see those words, 'John Perkins,' I feel good. It's not seeing my name as the director of an organization where my name has to be exalted to the public for fundraising purposes, it's seeing the hand of Christ at work through very painful years."

Having a child with polio, experiencing a near-broken marriage a few times, having to overcome speech impediments and learning to read in his early 20s, encountering rejection by the Church for many years, enduring and surviving the trying years that included Brandon jail—these were all "part of the privilege of having fellowship with Christ. He took on a human form and endured suffering unto death for my sake. Participating with His pain for the world's sake today is a very small way of saying thank you."

10

Family in Focus

I'M SOLD OUT to the ministry God called us to start. Anytime. Day, morning, night, I'm ready to do what I have to because I know this is right. There's no job too easy, too hard, too dirty or too plain for John and me. We do it all. Working together like that is just good. Sometimes John will say to me, 'Vera Mae, I don't think there is any fight we can't take on together.' Sometimes I don't want to stay, but we are not our own; we 'are bought with a price,' and so I have to stay. It's good and it's easy and it's hard."

Vera Mae is currently working on a book that will reflect her path of discipleship over the past 35 years. One thing is certain, without the book having yet been written, Vera Mae and John have fought the battle *together,* and one day they'll pick up crowns of equal glory. Vera Mae's story belongs in her book however, so we turn to John to ask the question, How would you describe your marriage?

"Explosive. We clash. Our personalities totally clash. The things she naturally likes I don't like. The things I naturally like she doesn't like."

John smiles his biggest smile as he talks of the intricacies of such a relationship. "I tend to be a highly freedom-oriented person; Vera Mae wants to control everything.

That's why she's in charge of the money. All the principles of what's supposed to make a good match for marriage aren't part of our reality. But we've been a family for 35 years and we've been successful."

Any big decision is mutual. If not, the explosive quotient goes to work. John and Vera Mae will "reason" together regarding those decisions. "Some people say that marriage is give and take—give a little, take a little. For us it's been a matter of reasoning together, arriving at a decision we both feel is reasonable."

They will often reject each other's idea at the outset and then allow themselves to be "reasoned with." A case in point is John's desire for an amphitheater on their Harambee Christian Family Center property. He could envision holding plays, shows, musical concerts and special education programs for community kids, if they would build an outdoor amphitheater on the property.

The decision was arrived at something like this:

John: Vera Mae, I've been thinking about building an amphitheater. It would be a great place for the kids.

Vera Mae: Absolutely not. First, you'll never get a builder's permit and, second, our insurance rates would go way up because of the danger it would pose to kids.

John: Okay. Let me think about it.

The next morning the subject is introduced again.

John: Vera Mae, I think I'm going to build an amphitheater.

Vera Mae: What would you do with an amphitheater?

John: Care for the kids in our community, get them off the streets.

Vera Mae: Hmmm. Let me think about it.

About the fourth round, John takes her out to the place he's been considering for the project.

Vera Mae: I still don't like it.

*All the principles of what's supposed
to make a good match for marriage
aren't part of our reality.
But we've been a family for 35 years
and we've been successful.*

A week later, standing at the site again:

John: Can't you see 200 kids here doing all sorts of good things?

Vera Mae: The amphitheater may not be such a bad idea. (Translation: I'm convinced, go ahead and build.)

They went through the same process recently for remodeling the kitchen. John had given the "may not be such a bad idea" signal the morning he left town for several speaking engagements. When he came back he found a new kitchen. Yet he had given a flat no when the idea first emerged.

"Our life has been hard all the way through. We accept that as our pattern. The calling we were given to pioneer community development during the 1960s was a difficult calling. But that was our reality. We've learned to work through any obstacle together, and we respect each other a great deal."

Being a husband and father was something John never witnessed growing up. He had no clues what sort of responsibilities went with it, he just understood the deep emotional bond he felt that day Jap hugged him and told him he loved him.

"I've had to learn what it means to be a father, and I guess I'd say I'm proud of how my children are living their lives."

John watched some godly men closely during his early days in Mendenhall, trying to learn their fatherly virtues. Parenting is learned "as you parent" says John, and not in a seminar somewhere. "You have to be committed to doing whatever you know and constantly reflect on the models about you."

Giving his children a purpose for life and a freedom to find God's call for their own futures are among the highest priorities John has had in parenting. He wants to give them

66

Our life has been hard all the way through.
We accept that as our pattern.
The calling we were given to pioneer
community development during the 1960s
was a difficult calling.
But that was our reality.
We've learned to work through
any obstacle together,
and we respect each other
a great deal.

99

a love for work, a desire to contribute to the well-being of society, a deep love for God. "I've also realized that one of the best ways to help society is to raise your children with godly lives. They go into society when they're all grown and contribute their lives to it with all that means in Christ."

During the early days of ministry in Mendenhall, before the unpredictable civil rights clashes totally disrupted family routines, John and Vera Mae woke the kids early six days each week and took them through Bible study, prayer and singing before they even had breakfast. Any time a community meeting was held, which could be as many as five nights each week, the kids attended.

"You didn't even have to give me the title of the hymn we were going to sing. Just say the page number, and I was all ready to go. We had those hymnbooks memorized like our Bibles," Derek recalls.

The Perkinses have eight children in all, all grown and all in love with the Lord. They admire their daddy, and Derek sums it up for them: "I want to serve my daddy as long as he lives. He's a man of God with a calling to the Church, and we need to help him, however we can."

John and Vera Mae had been separated for seven months when Spencer, the oldest child, was born in 1954. Eight months later, they moved together again to relaunch a very shaky marriage. Thanks to the sincere efforts of little Spencer who asked his daddy to come to Sunday School to learn about Jesus, John walked into the Kingdom with a five-year-old pushing from behind.

There were two daddies to Spencer—the pre-Brandon one and the post-Brandon daddy. He saw his dad age and grow somber through that time and, as a 16-year-old, was required to carry a lot of responsibility and pain that would have been hard on anyone that age.

> I've realized that one of the best ways
> to help society
> is to raise your children
> with godly lives.
> They go into society
> when they're all grown
> and contribute their lives to it
> with all that means in Christ.

"I was in eleventh grade when my daddy went through that. After his heart attack, I got a note from him in the hospital—he was telling me to be strong in life, to take care of Momma and to help my brothers and sisters make it through school. He was sure he was going to die, and I was being told that I was now the man of the house."

Spencer made All-state as a basketball player. His dad saw him play only once during his entire university career. Consequently, Spencer attended all of Phillip's and Derek's football games. With insight, he explains, "Dad had a call on his life. He knew what he was supposed to do, and he did it. I understood that clearer than ever when he got beat up in that prison."

Although Spencer went through a rebellious stretch in college while experiencing certain adolescent freedoms for the first time, he's firmly rooted in Jesus and is planning to do just as his father does: "Take the Word of God seriously, whether or not others follow it, and do what's right."

Spencer can remember his dad escaping to the bathroom for some private Bible reading and prayer. "I could always hear him mumbling in there. I have great respect for John Perkins, for the life he modeled and passed on to us."

Joanie is the loud child in the family. Rebellious, much like the early John Perkins, she didn't want anyone to control her life. In her memory, family life, between 1968 and 1972, seemed pretty much to have lost all its form. That served her independent spirit well, as she distanced herself from parental control as much as possible. Now Joanie works full-time at Voice of Calvary and seems cut out for leadership.

Derek found the period from 1968 to 1971 particularly painful, as he saw the struggles his dad went through

because of white oppression. Trying to reconcile the injustices of white Christians with the gospel, he began to hate whites and drifted away from the faith.

In 1979, while studying at Jackson State University, he realized that the cost his dad had paid by the way he lived was what the gospel was all about. He gave himself fully to Christ and is committed to being faithful to the simple but radical demands of the gospel.

Wayne and Phillip are the most introverted of the bunch. With tender hearts and high respect for their dad, they aren't always sure in their minds if they really please him. Phillip works in his brother's mechanics shop in Jackson, and Wayne runs the printing business located in the Harambee Christian Family Center in Pasadena.

Derek, Spencer and Joanie have moved into a community house which they hope will be a part of bringing the reconciling goodness of Jesus to Jackson.

Still living at home and working with the Christian Family Center in Pasadena are Debbie and Priscilla. Betty is studying at Pasadena City College to be a nurse.

The children all concur that John is not the perfect dad. But they also think it may be difficult to find a better one anywhere else. They've accepted that he was called to engage in a specific historical transition, and they respect his tenacity in seeing his role through to the end of that difficult time.

They have memories of a packed home; of people who came to join in the gospel cause sleeping all over the floor; of Bible memory, prayer and rallies; of hecklers and the fear of losing their daddy to white police. They can look back now and see that they were groomed for service and taught to think freely. They all respect the Word highly and have been trained to "call a spade a spade."

They see a dad who doesn't put his financial concerns

before his calling. They don't see him getting rich off his ministry. "We've learned that success isn't money," says Spencer. "It is being totally committed to whatever God calls you to do."

They've watched their dad learn to forgive his oppressors and then call others to join him as he actively tries to love them. They've seen him admit his wrongs, make drastic changes in his behavior, apologize, listen to critiques from others and continue to learn in a posture of humility.

John's children have learned from their daddy that all that counts is following Jesus and taking Him seriously in everything He commands. "Joy is knowing we're doing what we're supposed to be doing," says Derek. "Anything else is a dead-end street. It may not always be the *happy* thing to do, but it will be right."

11

Leader

JESUS LOOKED OUT at the crowds and saw them as 'sheep without a shepherd.' Right now society is in a mess, people are on their way to hell, and they don't know what to do about it. That's the shepherds' fault—the leaders' fault. If the shepherds would just shape up, so would the sheep.

"We have to be honest with ourselves. If society is in a mess, it's because the leaders are in a mess. I say we ought to be ashamed to be seen in our clerical collars."

John's hard-line view on leadership is consistent with his outlook on the rest of life. He takes his calling to leadership as a holy trust and believes that leaders who make their calling anything less than that have some "serious reckoning to do one day."

Leadership styles differ to be sure. John's school of leadership training was the civil rights movement. There were clearly the good guys and the bad guys. The enemy was out there and easy to define. There were no gray areas. Everything was in black and white. Issues were polarized and crises were created in order to get people to move.

That influence has stayed with John. "I demand absolute loyalty to my vision and ideals. If you question my commitment to Christ, to people, to the poor; if your life-style doesn't reasonably reflect what I'm about, then you're out. There's no place in our organization—not even for a day."

Some have harshly criticized John for this posture and have accused him of chewing up and spitting out some very sincere people.

"I don't doubt that in many cases I failed. But a leader has to accept that one of his great pains is going to be pop-ulating graveyards—asking people to resign. If I could go back and resurrect all those people I would. But I can't. That's the agony in leadership.

"A leader can accept incompetence. That's a difficult issue. If you want to take the time to train someone in cer-tain skill areas because they already buy your vision, that's a management decision. But move them on the minute they question your vision. There's some other place they can serve."

Living with peoples' judgment is just part of the price a leader has to accept. "The stories eventually get back to me that I simply lost patience or gave up on someone—that I was too idealistic and hacked a person out when I should have taken the time to let the vision mature."

But if John is demanding of people with the vision, he's demanding of himself with management skills. Those who have replaced him in the several ministries he started are unified in praising him for his ability to let go when the min-istry outgrows him. That quality is not taught in the lead-ership school of the civil rights movement, and it is to John's credit that he was able to discern the times.

"When I see need for someone else to be captain of the ship I need to be committed enough to the vision to get out of the way. My personal being shouldn't play into the ques-

66

Jesus looked out at the crowds
and saw them as 'sheep without a shepherd.'
Right now society is in a mess,
people are on their way to hell,
and they don't know what to do about it.
That's the shepherds' fault—
the leaders' fault.
If the shepherds would just shape up,
so would the sheep.

99

tion. For it's not a reflection of who I am; it's simply a statement about my skills and about the fact that our ministry has been blessed with growth beyond my capabilities. The vision, the people and the product are all much more important than the leader holding onto a position."

John believes that organizations have to adjust as the times change. A good leader is willing to take an organization through changes that reflect his own growth and understanding of the world. If he's unable to adjust his own thinking about reality from time to time and to let that shift reflect itself in the organization, then he's built a stable structure that is sure to lose its ability to serve society.

How does a leader get started?

"Opportunity is a door that opens before you. You're able to understand what's on the other side of that door and how stepping through it will serve society. The leader is able to step through that door, develop the product and deliver it to those who will be served by it. Those who can never make it through those doors are not leaders."

Just as truth is what's lived out, for John, leadership is de facto. If you are a leader, then you're a leader.

"The other side of this leadership picture is understanding that it's time to pass through the door—to understand that you're no longer the person meant to deliver that particular package to society."

A leader is also capable of surrounding himself with others of complementary skills. A dependency is formed where people lean on each other's expertise.

John likes to tell the story of his visiting Patterson Air Force Base to speak at the Officers Club: "The chief chaplain took me to meet the commander of the base. He was black. Just after we sat down in his office, an emergency call came to him over his intercom. The airbase tower told him that a plane with a crew of six had been having difficulty lowering its landing gear. While circling the base several times to rectify the situation they had run out of fuel.

"The question was, What to do with the jet? Technically, it was the commander's jet, and he should decide if it should be ditched. I watched as the commander asked to be put in touch with the crew. He asked the pilot his background and then that of each of the other crew members. Rogers told them they were better equipped with their training to make the decision. We watched as they brought the plane in for a safe landing."

John concludes, "People who know the most about the product should be making the decisions regarding that product."

Roland Hinz was particularly attracted to John on this level. "He attracts a unique group of people, a very broad constituency of supporters. He's able to fill his board of directors with specialists such as medical people, Ph.D.s and pastors and mix them with the lowest level people who may not have professional training but who understand the society the organization is committed to serving."

Also important to Roland is John's teachability and humility. "I saw immediately that here was a good strong leader who knew where he was going, but I also discovered a man who is reasonable. We've had several discussions where I just don't agree with some of his programs or ideas. At times he'll come back to me and say, 'Roland, you have a good point there,' and he'll completely abandon the initiative. Not many leaders are willing to listen to others."

The Church has boxed that sensitivity out of the pastor's role according to John. The pastor is the superstar of the congregation: He knows everything better than anyone else, has a special line to God for input and owns a cor-

> *The servant-leader is conscious of his own sinfulness and brokenness and will look for people who can communicate those weaknesses to him.*

ner on revelation. "All I need to do as pastor is to go to my room, bow my head, and God is going to tell me everything that is necessary. Well, that's not exactly what happened with David. It took the prophet Nathan to confront him with his adulterous relationship with Bathsheba before he was able to come to grips with it. The servant-leader is conscious of his own sinfulness and brokenness and will look for people who can communicate those weaknesses to him."

Another leadership principle has to do with motivation. The pastor who blames his congregation for not being more in step with his vision lacks the insight to note that the members are simply reflecting his own inability to lead. The leader's report card is the people under him. "If you take on a piece of society and after a time it doesn't look any different, you need to begin asking some tough questions about your calling to lead in that place.

"Much of leadership is team playing. One day the coach comes into the locker room and discovers that he can't motivate the players any more. That happens. It's time for a decision. Either the coach leaves, or the coach moves some of the players along.

"It's only natural that some people will outgrow their calling to a certain ministry. But it's also possible that some people shouldn't have been there in the first place. That's the leader's responsibility, and he should move those people or himself on as soon as he realizes the mistake.

"The leader is absolutely responsible for the whole. Some people who work under the leader are irresponsible in their duties, but the leader is even responsible for that. The leader can never ultimately live with the comfort that 'someone else was responsible.' It's another one of those pains that go with the calling."

John has regularly encountered what he calls the "ego demon" in people who come to work under him but who are not secure in their own frailties. They're unwilling to seek help in the areas of their responsibilities where they're failing, because they think that's a poor reflection of their self-worth. "These are mean people to have around you. They're provincial—don't want you to get too close to their job, don't want to be held very accountable. When you start asking questions they become defensive." People who suffer with the "ego demon" have self-destruction built in. Their pride blinds them and they think they would do much better if the leader would just step aside.

Being a third-grade dropout has been a benefit to John in this regard. People aren't quick to trust his abilities, so he has to demonstrate that results are forthcoming. He lives in a society that tells him every day that he doesn't amount to much. No sheepskins on the wall to prove his worth. "Even though I can point to honorary doctorates, I have this gnawing inside that I didn't get society's passport. But on the other hand I experience a deep sense of satisfaction that society couldn't hold me back."

Leaders are also distinguished by their ability to make decisions. "I know few people under 35 years old who I would say are qualified to be good leaders—there hasn't been enough time for them to make decisions and reflect on their consequences."

People who are scared of making decisions or who can't make them quickly will not make good leaders. "Decisions cannot be procrastinated. Some of our decisions are made by not making a decision. That shows our weakness to take a stand and live with the consequences. A leader has the internal stamina to say, 'I took action and I stand accountable for the results.'"

"

*When I see a need for someone else
to be captain of the ship
I need to be committed enough
to the vision to get out of the way.
My personal being shouldn't play into the
question.
For it's not a reflection of who I am;
it's simply a statement about my skills
and about the fact that our ministry
has been blessed with growth
beyond my capabilities.
The vision, the people and the product
are all much more important
than the leader holding onto a position.*

"

Living with people's criticisms is a part of decision-making. A good leader knows he's human but he knows his calling. He's willing to lead for the sake of his calling and he's not crushed when the result shows the decision to be a poor choice. A lesson is learned and the leader moves forward better equipped for the next round.

Ultimately, a leader is one who has accepted a burden, has decided to take responsibility for one of society's woes. The Christian leader is able to get those cues from God. "That leader is a man of understanding. He's a thinker. He argues with the world out there because it doesn't reflect God's desires. He's not captivated by its values, pursuits or promises. He sees through that; he's able to discern what the gods of this world are. Today it may be materialism; tomorrow, who knows. But that's the strength of a leader—he's not stuck in a groove, he's constantly interacting."

The leader who is constrained by God doesn't stop with understanding alone. His understanding becomes his burden, his calling. He's moved to compassion by the Holy Spirit to organize his energies and skills in such a way that society will benefit from his understanding.

"This takes faith. It's the ability to see a future that isn't there. It's a hope, an expectation deep down in your guts that there will be results. It's the sort of hope that moved Abraham to his journey, the sort of hope that stirred the Israelites to carry Joseph's bones with them to the other side of Canaan.

"The leader has the ability to live out that hope whether or not anyone is willing to go for the ride. This sort of leadership is a spirit, a conviction that prompts you to prepare your future around the hope. And the really mature leader is one who can believe that the next generation will benefit from the results, even if he's not there to see it. You so believe in the worth of what you're doing you can accept in your heart that society will be the better for it. So you don't live to experience those fruits yourself, you live by faith that some day someone will experience the fruit."

John's life is unquestionably a living demonstration of those principles he's come to believe.

He has a burden. It's a society that doesn't know its daddy, that is beset with fears, loneliness, alienation, hatred. He carries a weight of responsibility for that parentless society. He knows the Father and the Father has given him understanding—he's not free to walk away from it. He has a vision, a plan, a means that sees society cared for. He's moving into the areas of pain and allowing them to become his very own. He has identified with the hurt and is moved by compassion, because the victims are real people.

And he's persevered. His personal walk with his Father gives him the courage and the strength to hold on through the afflictions of discipline, the criticisms and naysayers, the personal failures and deep longings. He truly has a dream that no one can take from him, and when he gets up tomorrow morning he'll launch out once again for that city that is not of this world. In the meanwhile, the world will become a better place because of it.

12

God, the Lord

IS IT POSSIBLE that John Perkins just might be, at heart, a closet communist? Does his insistence on redistribution as one of the pillars of his 3 *R*s suggest, as some have hinted, that John advocates a thinly disguised form of socialism? To such questions, his answer is always a resounding no.

"The free enterprise system—the capitalistic system—is probably the greatest production enterprise that's ever been created. I affirm the system and its principles, but that same system in the hands of wicked and greedy people can be just as deadly and wicked as socialism and communism.

"I think the great weakness in our free enterprise system is in its distribution, especially in terms of the people at the bottom. In that respect, our existing system lacks justice."

Justice, then—biblical justice—and not the imposition of another "ism" is what John Perkins is all about. Yet, in most evangelical circles, *justice* is a dirty word, conjuring up images of left-wing radicals who love Marxists a little more than capitalists, who embrace socialism rather than free enterprise, who are naive about the evils of Soviet

Russia and who are trying to force American Christians to give up their God-ordained right to self-determination.

The word "justice" is central to John's vocabulary and life. And his use of the word is a lot more radical than the usage evangelicals already fear. For John, *justice* is "the application of the biblical truth that everything belongs to God."

"One of the weaknesses of capitalism is that it doesn't believe God owns the world. There is no biblical idea that God ever gives us ownership of the earth or its resources.

"The earth is always 'the Lord's, and the fulness thereof.' Christians are called only to be *stewards* of His resources. Capitalistic people seem to think that as much as they can get hold of belongs to them. They manage it for their own high good and the good of those who helped them get it. But they don't consider God's view of how those same resources are meant to work for the people who are unable to sustain life, the people whose quality of life is dependent on the resources we control."

The most distinctive element of John's view of justice and, at the same time, probably the most disturbing for evangelicals in America is John's concept of individual ownership. John believes and affirms that God owns all of creation (see Ps. 24:1) and that He alone has the right to determine creation's usage. He delegates to His Church the holy trust of caring for those resources in a manner that reflects His desires for all people. And one day, He will call for an accounting of that trust (see Matt. 25:14-46; Rom. 14:11-12).

"God's creation is not just for the selfish few, but for the many. In suburban America we have a personalized Christianity—everything is for me. That is idolatry. We are supposed to be the prophetic people of God. We are meant to hold society accountable to a holy God."

66

There is no biblical idea
that God ever gives up
ownership of the earth
or its resources.
The earth is always 'the Lord's,
and the fulness thereof.'
Christians are called
only to be stewards
of His resources.

99

The Church's corporate life should give society both a standard for the righteousness of God and a stumbling block for the secular way of life. But instead, the Church has become hopelessly captivated by the standards of society. We have accepted both the view that our personal rights are central to our existence and the view that money will buy our way to attaining all the good that life can offer.

Consequently, we've become locked into capitalism and "the American way" because capitalism proves to be the best way to increase personal wealth. "But we've lost the understanding that it creates more wealth only for the few. It's not being distributed. And we lose sight of the fact that it doesn't belong to any of us anyway."

Despite the continuing risk of being labeled "socialist" or "anticapitalistic," John remains adamant that all the earth's resources be put to use according to God's pleasure. John is not against individual ownership. Rather, he calls for *biblical* individual ownership—which is to be viewed in terms of "how do I manage these assets that ultimately belong to God?"

The assimilation by evangelical Christians of conventional American views on individual ownership and personal rights impedes our ability to think biblically about justice. The result is that we twist the meaning of the word *justice* to accommodate our own selfish pursuits. To underscore his point, John states, "If I own a million barrels of shortening, and someone demands that I give him one of those barrels, I could protest that I'm being dealt a gross injustice, that my personal ownership rights are being violated. It doesn't matter that I don't need those million barrels or that the other person is struggling to survive. For me then, the issue is simply, 'Those are *my* barrels.'"

Justice, then, in the American vocabulary, is reduced to mean "the protection of my property, the defense of my individual ownership efforts."

John often reflects on the miniseries, "Roots." At one point, a young Christian is forced to make a decision. He was about to be married and needed to make enough money to set up his home. He contracted as a ship master and, just before fetching his cargo, discovered it was to be slaves. Confronted with the choice of forsaking the mistreatment of black human beings from Africa or of continuing the pursuit of his personal dreams, he chose the latter. "He compromised his Christianity to make a perfectly sound capitalistic decision: 'My pursuit of economic gain should not be limited by the effect it has on others.' That is still 'the American way' and we guard it fiercely with all sorts of biblical justifications."

Biblical justice, however, would demand that I not gain at the expense of others. It would ask how the personal development of resources impacted the larger community, how it impacted all of humanity for which Jesus died. A biblical understanding of "gain" would render the thought of increase-at-the-expense-of-others repulsive.

In protecting our personal pursuits, we spiritualize, in fact, almost deify the system of capitalism. We can find no wrong in it and so we find sanction to advance our ends unhindered. "We like to think that capitalism is good within itself. But it is good only in the hands of good men. There's nothing sanctified about it.

"Both systems are part of a fallen world; they're both basically from the devil. Capitalism, when permitted to run free without constraints on selfish interests, creates monopolies such as those we see operating today between North America and Latin America. We have created misery for those people affected."

*We like to think
that capitalism is good
within itself.
Capitalism is just as wicked
in the hands of wicked people
as communism is.
There's nothing sanctified
about it.*

John won't preach "anticommunism" sermons because he believes that is a luxury of the privileged. The oppressed black in the South was told during the '60s by whites that people who were demanding changes were actually communists. People in Central America who want to be free of their right-wing dictators are being told that such desires are communist-inspired. Blacks caught in the clutches of apartheid are being warned that all uprisings in the urban centers of South Africa are communist-directed.

"That sort of thought is only important to the powerful and the oppressor. Black families in Soweto would simply like to eat properly, get a good chance at life and find employment. They're not debating the high ideas of capitalism verses communism. It's only the folks fearing to lose their economic advantage over others who shun justice and talk of the threat of communism."

American Christianity, in John's view, is afraid of this sort of countercultural message. It is unable to separate itself from its culture enough to ask hard questions about justice. This is particularly true for the large Christian ministries that depend on a wide base of financial donors to operate. The golden rule is, "Don't offend the people with the big bank accounts. If our rich supporters preach anticommunism, we preach anticommunism. Our message is owned by them because our financial survival is linked to their generosity. If we question the validity of unlimited personal gain, we begin to sound anti-American to those magnates and we begin to question the very system that put them in their places of financial power."

Rather than endanger our financial base, we remain silent on the biblical call for justice. The rich donors win, and the gospel loses because we have denied the biblical fact that God is the Lord of His creation. We have adjusted the gospel to accommodate "the American way" rather than defending the gospel to assert the Lord's way.

It's easy to confuse justice with mercy. A Christian can look at the plight of black Sowetans and say, "Let's start a fund to give them more food and a better education." That would be an appropriate biblical response, because mercy is a Christian characteristic. But it doesn't ask about the structural system that keeps blacks in their oppressive situation.

"Justice looks for a way to guarantee *equal access* to life's resources at the earliest ages. It asks how to reduce the black infant mortality rate so that more blacks have access to life. It asks how to provide better nutrition so that young kids have equal access to their mental capacities, and it asks how a black kid can advance economically with the same advantages of the white kid. If there is some legal or other structural system in place that makes it more likely the white kid will advance, then you have an unjust system."

Distributing justice is similar to supplying water for a population. You develop a system that will deliver the water. You bring engineers together who can design and construct water channels that bring water within reach of those needing the water. They have access to it.

Some people are more motivated than others to use creatively the water in ways that will accomplish more. That's a question of gifting. The demand for justice, however, is satisfied when we have given people equal access to God's creation. "Justice is the helpman of God—helping humanity to have access to the Creation that God so lovingly provided for His created."

"The problem in South Africa is that the people who are native to the land don't have access to it. Because they do not have equal access to God's creation, they have no power, very little means to earn adequately and low moti-

vation. They have little incentive to believe that there is hope for their plight. They live in their ghettos, isolated in poverty and want, while we conservative Americans have the view that just maybe some day those white folks there who claim to be Christian will somehow decide to share the wealth.

"It is the Christian's duty to work for a creative solution to the plight of those deprived of open access to the resources of that land. But we ourselves are part of their problem, because we really don't believe God created the earth to benefit all humanity."

John believes that the American slogan of "liberty and justice *for all*" has become too costly a concept for those who have benefited from the liberty to pursue their individual wealth unchecked. He isn't naively looking at the American culture, believing that it can easily go through a change to live for the biblical vision of justice. Nor is his demand that the Church let go its grip on individual rights; rather, that the Church squarely face some hard questions: Do others have equal access to these rights? Do we really believe God to be the Lord? Does all creation belong to Him? Are we honestly, simply stewards of His resources, focusing all those resources on His desire to care for all of society with the same care He has shown each one of us?

John is brutally consistent in demanding that truth be evident in his own life. For truth, if it is to be made visible, if it is to be practically worked out in the natural world, requires that his life make a difference in some specific place in society.

And he places that same demand on the Church. Ultimately, it is the Church which has been given the mandate to be the radical instrument of God in bringing about the reign of God, the reign of justice in society.

66

*Justice
is the helpman of God—
helping humanity to have access
to the Creation that God
so lovingly provided
for His created.*

99

"The biblical Church is that group of people who have come together under the reconciling grace of Jesus to care for the world. They become the visible demonstration of the new justice relationships that can happen when the Spirit of God enters. They become the medium by which God reconciles people to Himself and each other. They begin to look rather strange in that they hold all things in common. No one in their midst is needy because those who have much sell their plenty to give to those who have nothing. It sounds a little bit like something you read about in the New Testament, doesn't it?"

John and Vera Mae have been the stewards of millions of dollars, 64 homes and dozens of public service businesses, but their asset sheet doesn't have a lot to show for it. In fact, the house they live in now in Pasadena is owned by the ministry and not by them.

In secular terms, they have let go of a place in society that is rightfully theirs. But in their minds they're building a home that's not in this world. People in Pasadena have been learning something about that home as they come under the caring parenting of the Perkinses; they're getting a vision of building their own.

13

Homestretch

EMBEDDED IN JOHN'S mind is the perspective that the last five minutes of his life could disqualify him from the race. What can he tell us about perseverance? "That's something I won't know anything about until my last breath. Perseverance is revealed at that final moment. If you have to assure me on my deathbed that I'm going to heaven, I will have lived my life in vain. It would suggest that I've lived some sort of lie—it would mean that someone back there tricked me theologically. If, in the home stretch, I have grown weary in doing the good Christ has shown me to do, I would have to accept that I had been living for a theological position rather than for the person of Jesus."

John's prayer is that he will go out of this life at full speed. Even though he believes in eternal security—and he has the confidence that his salvation is a gift from God that no one can take from him—he believes that, if he gives up at the very end, it would indicate that he never was a Christian to begin with.

"The thought of perseverance can't be measured in this life. It has to be pushed into the eternal state where I acknowledge that, if I'm saved, then the love of God, the

66

If you have to assure me
on my deathbed
that I'm going to heaven,
I will have lived
my life in vain.

99

power of His Spirit and the will He creates in me will have pushed me through to the end, so that I can then thankfully say, 'I have fought a good fight.' I didn't give up!"

This understanding of perseverance is married to John's life-style. Just as Abraham had to take an initial step of faith into the unknown and then venture into a daily walk that would see its fulfillment only in a future generation, John's initial step of faith toward Christ has become a daily journey of obedience and discipline that ends in the next life. It may be that some elect to give up on that daily journey before it enters the eternal. But not John.

"My hope won't be lost. My heavenly Father is going to carry me through that time of dying, no matter how painful it may be. I believe I will be saying that I did what I could, I did what was practical and I tried as hard as I could."

John's longings then will have finally been met. He will find himself at home with Daddy.

> *In God's own sovereign way,*
> *I end up feeling*
> *my life has been significant*
> *if I haven't made significance my goal.*
> *I will be able to see*
> *that my children love God*
> *and want to do His will.*
> *I will see*
> *that my neighborhood has changed*
> *and that people are believing*
> *in their own dignity and self-worth.*
> *I will see people*
> *who now have a Father*
> *and know they are really loved.*

To John Perkins
With best wishes,

Ronald Reagan

DON'T MISS
CRY JUSTICE!

NOW AVAILABLE in full-color 16 mm. film and video cassette, *CRY JUSTICE,* the dramatic, challenging life-story of John Perkins. Based on *Let Justice Roll Down,* John's own moving autobiography, this stirring cinematic presentation of victory through Christ over tragedy, poverty and injustice is available for both private and public viewing.

Video purchase (DG174): $49.95

Video rental (DR174): $30.00

Film (rental only): $75.00

To place an order or to obtain further details call Gospel Light Video today. From outside California call 1-800-235-3415. From inside California, call 1-800-227-4025.

Also obtainable from Gospel Light Video are three of John Perkins' most powerful messages on Christian Community Development:

CHRISTIAN COMMUNITY DEVELOPMENT	LENGTH	RENTAL FEE	PURCHASE PRICE	CODE
THE FELT NEED CONCEPT	45 MIN.	$20.00	$24.95	DGV13
CHURCH'S RESPONSIBILITY TO THE POOR	45 MIN.	$20.00	$24.95	DGV14
LEADERSHIP FOR TODAY	45 MIN.	$20.00	$24.95	DGV15
CHRISTIAN COMMUNITY DEVELOPMENT SERIES	3 MSGS.	$49.00 (4 WKS)	$60.00	DZM08

Order now from Gospel Light Video.

Maye A Hardin
919 Bluestone Rd
Durham NC 27713

John Perkins. A man—

> At war with the world
> At peace with his Lord
> At odds with the Church
> At home with the poor.